LIVE
the Life
you Long for

Annie Evans' journey began when she was diagnosed with inoperable cancer. With nothing to lose she decided to find out all she could about healing and apply it to her life. Her discoveries about life-energy amazed her. Annie is now a highly respected energetic and spiritual healer, and a lecturer at a leading Sydney college of natural therapies.

LIVE the Life you Long for

Healing your family, work and relationship issues

ANNIE EVANS

ALLEN&UNWIN

First published in 2010

Copyright © Annie Evans 2010

Inspired Living, an imprint of
Allen & Unwin
83 Alexander Street
Crows Nest NSW 2065
Australia
Phone: (61 2) 8425 0100
Fax: (61 2) 9906 2218
Email: info@allenandunwin.com
Web: www.allenandunwin.com

Cataloguing-in-Publication details are available
from the National Library of Australia
www.librariesaustralia.nla.gov.au

ISBN 978 1 74175 946 4

Internal design by Bookhouse, Sydney
Internal illustrations by Squirt Creative
Set in 12.25/17 pt Dante by Bookhouse, Sydney
Printed and bound in Australia by Griffin Press

10 9 8 7 6 5 4 3 2 1

Praise for Annie Evans' work

Annie, the generous way you open yourself up, share your knowledge, talk about your experiences and unusual happenings along the way, inspires others to feel safe to explore their own journey.

Suzie

Annie, thank you for your enthusiasm, wisdom and 'Annie' stories about energetic healing. You have sparked curiosity within me to gain further knowledge about this area of life. You have inspired me to continue along this exciting pathway.

Wendy

Thank you, Annie, for your support, guidance, love, wisdom, encouragement, time and simply your presence.

Meaghan

You are inspirational.

Mahal

Thank you so much, Annie, for being such a big part of our lives, and for your constant love, understanding and support.

Nicole and Frank

Annie, I feel so compelled to write to you to thank you for all you have released in me. After our session I can honestly say that my life has turned around. I credit you for enabling this. Your kindness, wisdom and generosity of spirit are a gift to all of us in this world. You arrived in my life at just the right moment and I thank my lucky stars for presenting you to me.

Lisa

Annie, gratitude for your insightful teachings, your abundant wisdom and the free flowing gift of yourself. Thank you for being you.

Janet

Annie, I would like to thank you for all your support, guidance, wisdom and kindness.

Kelly

You are an incredible bright, shining beacon of light. You allow others to uncover and find their own light and truth in your reflection. Thank you for all that you are.

Monique

This course has been the beginning of a life-changing journey for me. I would like to thank you for being a wonderful and fun teacher.

Kathy

Dedicated to my parents and loving husband, Bob.
You have been my greatest teachers.

To my children
Randall, Bradley and Loucia.
I love you.

To my grandchildren
Tahlia, Zoe, Lauren, Mae and Azalea.
Thank you for graciously allowing my aliases
'Ninny' and 'Nannie' to simply be and play.

To my brother, Robert, and dearest Uncle Brian.
Thank you for playing your role in my journey.

Loving kindness to you all.

Acknowledgements

Gratitude does not express the patience and kindness of my publisher Maggie Hamilton, who made manifest the seed for this book three years ago. She embodies the gift of loving kindness, with her abundant dedication and understanding of the uninitiated author's journey. In a role not dissimilar to that of a midwife, Maggie professionally and passionately sets about bringing work such as this to the light of day, raising the consciousness of the collective.

To Margaret Spicer, who had the gift of intuitive insight and her collaboration with Martine Negro to bring a course in energy healing and consciousness together in the Diploma of Energetic and Spiritual Healing, I am truly grateful. You opened the door to my destined path.

It was with great trepidation, excitement and fear that I took a leap of faith into the unknown, following the road less traveled. Now I look back and see how the journey was *so* perfect—thank God I trusted!

To all those people who have known the patterns of pain and suffering in their life, I honour and dedicate this work to you. Through synchronicity and divine timing I hope my story will inspire your spirit to unlock the healing power within. I wish you light and love as you find your way home.

To those dear friends, students and teachers that I have met along the way, each one of you has served me beautifully, showing me where I have needed to grow and not be afraid to love. I am gratefully humble.

To Lizzie, a true soul mate, the support, love and impact you've had on my life is beyond words—blessings always. To Angela Rossmanith, or AA as I would affectionately call her, without your brilliant writing and editing skills this book may have never made it to the birthing process; I am humbly filled with gratitude. To Scott Dunstan, for your support and initial creative input to this book, thank you. To Ann Lennox, I have loved your in-house editing efficiency and ideas; it has been a pleasure to work with you. To Megan Johnston, thank you for your copyediting skills and sensitivity to work of this kind. It was graciously appreciated. Thanks also to Robyn Vincent, who always managed to share her computer skills and light just at the right time, and Jeanette Young for 'checking in' when my spirit needed lifting. Love to you all.

Blessings,
Annie

Contents

Introduction

I am an energetic healer and teacher who assists people to find their own way to self-healing through intuitive counselling and a host of other energy healing tools. When I read a person's energy clairvoyantly, and attune to their inner dialogue, I can connect with their hidden cellular memory patterns. Discovering these patterns opens the doorway to so much information and personal transformation.

All my work is focused around life-energy—something that has fascinated me since I was a young girl, yet for many years I was a sceptic. Then, during a difficult time in my life, crossing the boundaries of life and death three times, I accepted responsibility for my own self-healing, took a leap of faith, and discovered a whole new world. My pain and suffering literally changed my life.

When I began this journey I knew very little about the power of life-energy, about auras and chakras, and the way old patterns keep us stuck and make us sick. I'd no idea about the law of attraction or how our bodies' cells have memory, about the healing power of love, forgiveness and personal truth. In my search for the meaning to life's greater plan I began studying the ancient wisdom teachings, eastern and western mysticism and spirituality. I also explored the unseen world of spirit.

In this book I share with you all the amazing things I have discovered. I invite you to join me on a wonderful journey that will forever change how you see yourself and others. As I share some of my own stories you will see how I've put energetic healing into practice in my daily life and how transforming that can be. My hope is that you can then apply these approaches to your own life and enjoy abundant wellbeing.

Love and blessings to you.

1
Joy and grief

I'll never forget the day in 1984 I received a letter telling us that we could adopt a little girl from Sri Lanka. It was something we'd been waiting for for a very long time.

The plan was that my mother and our two young sons would travel with us to Sri Lanka. But then, just days before we were to leave, my mother suffered deep abdominal pain. She told us she could not make the journey and that she could only look after our boys for a short time while we were away.

With heavy hearts we had to make new plans, and quickly. Family friends agreed to take in our boys. We repacked their suitcases, replacing the cool holiday clothes with all the school and sports gear they would now need. The boys had been looking forward to our holiday adventure. So, as we repacked their suitcases, I wrote little messages of love and support, hugs and kisses to scatter among their clothes, reminders of the exciting event that was about to happen on our arrival home.

Even though inter-country adoptions were uncommon and tricky at that time, for me it was fulfilling a childhood vision. And now as Bob an I set off for Sri Lanka, the small teardrop shaped country nestled just below India, I felt as though my stomach had been invaded by a thousand butterflies.

The dawn of each new day in Sri Lanka brought joy and excitement as we rose early to the honking horns of the tuk-tuks and the burring noise of the government buses whizzing past our hotel window.

There were schedules to meet, legal documentation to execute, challenges and language barriers to overcome. We were three weeks into our Sri Lankan adventure now and it didn't take us long to realise that adopting a child in a foreign country wasn't a straightforward process. We had to work around the restricted business hours of the Sri Lankan government departments. The queues and traffic were endless. Our lack of local language and the frenzy of a country on the brink of civil war added to the mixed mayhem and confusion we felt at times.

What a special day it was when we went to the embassy to pick up our new little daughter's passport. It was our first official photo. I clearly remember sitting on the edge of the bed in our hotel room staring and smiling, in fact you couldn't wipe the smile and joy off our faces. Her name was Loucia. We could hardly believe how lucky we were.

Although we'd been told originally that we would be adopting a child anywhere between birth and eighteen months, Loucia was almost seven years old. Her age fitted perfectly with that of our two boys, nine and twelve. Loucia's family had chosen adoption due to their extreme poverty.

The day at the courthouse is seared in my memory. I can only guess how her parents must have felt giving their little daughter away. After the finalisation of all court procedures we took Loucia back to our hotel. To mark the special occasion, we presented her with a pair of gold earrings we'd had especially made in a typical Sri Lankan style. It was a new beginning for us all.

We called my mother to share our excitement about Loucia but her voice sounded small and distant. I was acutely aware that something was up and knew that it was nothing to do with our boys. Mum had felt like an outcast all her life due to her unusually dark olive skin and less than ideal beginnings. As a child, Mum had been called all sorts of names because she looked different. All those buried feelings of shame, worthlessness and insecurity were now coming to the surface for her.

What hadn't helped was that we had moved house recently from a beachside suburb near Mum to a tree-lined bush estate much further away. Sadly, Mum felt the distance between us and didn't like it. She wanted me to mother her and couldn't understand why I wanted to adopt a little girl.

We were happy to return home to introduce our beautiful new daughter to her brothers, her extended family and friends. Loucia gave a huge smile at all the balloons and gifts presented to her. Mum tried to smile, but it was forced. She didn't appear well at all.

Over the next few months her health deteriorated. At the end of the year she had her gall bladder removed. She lost a lot of weight, felt miserable and depressed and became fearful about leaving the house. Mum had lost her confidence.

As well as returning to work, undergoing another house move to accommodate our growing family, and settling our daughter into her new country, Mum had become more physically and emotionally dependent on me. It felt overwhelming some days. Mum mirrored the struggle of a small group of family and friends who had difficulty accepting our adoption process. Bob and I couldn't believe the bigoted views that emerged! It brought us closer to understanding that what appeared to be loving, normal and natural for us was forging into new unexplored territories and pushing social boundaries with family and so-called friends. Some days I would sob with sadness and frustration.

Mum was referred to psychiatrists for counselling, but refused to go because it was personally too threatening for her. I pleaded with her to get help, but she wouldn't listen. It was obvious to me that her difficult past was a key to her health problems, but she shut herself off from any help. By now my poor mum was in and out of hospital, undergoing tests and seeing doctors. During surgery to investigate a blockage in the pancreas, they discovered pancreatic cancer. I was with her when the doctor delivered the news. He told my mother that she had six months at most to live. He could offer chemotherapy to keep her comfortable for a while, nothing more. Then, with Mum and me sitting opposite him in total shock, he went on to discuss the new position to which he had just been appointed in another state. He would arrange for a new doctor to take over my mother's case, he said, and showed us out of his office.

My mother and I walked out in horror and disbelief. We both felt so much fear and rage. A death sentence delivered just like that. No empathy, no compassion. We were on our own. Soon afterwards, Bob left to take up a new position in another city. The children and I were to follow him once he had made suitable arrangements.

Sadly, Mum became more and more dependent, and moved in with me. Her deep anger, fear of death, overwhelming anxiety and unwillingness to change or to see another perspective were very clear. She did not want to take responsibility for anything and was continuing to deny the emotional turmoil in her life.

Feeling desperate, I started to look around for alternative therapies. I'd heard there might be different ways to deal with cancer, and I wanted to know what they were. Someone told us about Dr Ainslie Meares, a remarkable man known for teaching meditation to cancer patients to help them relax. He was a pioneer in teaching that disease is not only physical, but that your mind, body and spirit all contribute to ill health. He believed anxiety and stress impaired our quality of life more than anything else and that they made pain feel far worse.

After talking with us and listening to Mum, Dr Meares said that my mother was gravely ill and he was unable to help her. He made a valuable suggestion, though, that we learn to meditate. Mum and I would go to his rooms and sit in large, comfortable recliner chairs, and Dr Meares would lead us into a relaxed state. He would encourage us to focus on our breathing, to move more slowly in everything we did, telling us how important it was to slow down the whole process of life. After our sessions with him, as we walked across the park towards our hotel, he would watch the way we walked and yell out, 'Slower! Slower!'

Learning to relax and to meditate helped me cope with looking after three children alone and with Mum dying and very angry. It was a terribly difficult time. My mother had feared cancer all her life. She'd always had the idea that you couldn't touch people with cancer, that somehow it was catching. Now she had it herself, and she was enraged.

Mum died just a couple of years after we had come home full of joy with our little daughter. On the day we buried Mum, I left for a new life with my husband and children in a new city.

2

A wake-up call

Life is a complex business. Once we'd moved I thought I could leave the past behind and dared to feel excited about the future. Yet, despite the sense of having made a great escape after the last six months, we had many new challenges. Finding suitable rented accommodation didn't prove easy. New schools for the children brought long travel challenges in peak-hour traffic on unfamiliar roads. I also needed to deal with Mum's belongings, sell her house, pack up our old house and rent it out. That meant travelling back and forth between cities, and I began to feel spread thin. I became exhausted mentally, emotionally and physically.

Within two weeks of Mum's death I had a suspected cancer removed from my right breast. Another shock! I woke from the anaesthetic to find I still had both breasts—and was immensely relieved. But I felt a deep void in my heart, what seemed a bottomless pit of sadness. There was nothing in my life that gave me any sense of safety, joy or happiness. Over the span of five years we ended up moving six times. That's a lot of moving, especially with three kids. And my husband's new job took him overseas for weeks on end. Alone and with no support, I felt totally drained. I had no time to grieve the loss of my mum and found myself teary one minute, angry the next, then totally overwhelmed.

I yearned for love. I wanted to cry, be rocked, to be held. I couldn't reach out for love or even recognise it. Instead, I felt a chilling coldness at the core of me. Parts of me were still back in my old home, while I was physically functioning in this new city. It was a strange feeling, as though I was dismembered.

I realise now that I was grieving not only for my mum but for all the deaths of my loved ones and the many changes that had taken place in my life. I felt fearful, sad and depressed, although I didn't understand that fully at the time. Even the everyday task of grocery shopping made me cry. I missed my mum, the simple things we used to do together. I couldn't walk down the pet-food aisle at the supermarket because we'd had to put our beloved dog into the pound—no-one would rent us a house if we had animals.

My confidence and self-worth were at an all-time low. During this time I had a hysterectomy and repairs to a hole in my bladder. I was experiencing loss on so many different levels. My recovery gave me time off from my part-time work. I'd hoped for a bit of a break, but instead spent all my time looking for a permanent house for the family. A few months afterwards my father-in-law died. We'd been close, and he was like my own father who'd died many years before. Another loss.

Then, just after my thirty-ninth birthday, I was diagnosed with non-Hodgkin's lymphoma. I had an inoperable cancer with a five per cent survival rate. Suddenly I was confronted with my own mortality, and knew how my mother must have felt. At the same time I saw that my mother's experience was a gift. I decided to put the terrible fear of cancer to rest and not accept the diagnosis as a death sentence. It was a huge hurdle to come to that decision.

I respected the amazing work doctors do but I knew I had to overhaul my life and make the changes that were urgently needed. That meant understanding the underlying causes of my cancer, looking at the recurring emotional and mental patterns in my life at the time of my diagnosis. I knew I was out of balance in my body, mind and spirit. As I began to look back at my life I saw how for years the painful, unresolved issues between my mother and myself had distanced me from self-love, literally closing my heart. Something had to change, but it wasn't until I was diagnosed with cancer that I realised just how much change was needed.

Suddenly I could see how I had attracted this disease to my body through years of hurt and negativity. It may sound strange but the more you dwell on something, the more it seems to be in your life. Now I was determined to do what was necessary to eliminate the disease. I wanted to attract good health, and that meant a new way of thinking.

While I wanted to explore other approaches, I agreed to chemotherapy. The haematology department of the hospital had been trialling a particular type of chemotherapy for the cell-type of my lymphoma. The doctors told me it would be administered over three months. I'd have a month off before I underwent radiotherapy.

It was a horrible time. I feel sorry for anyone who has to undergo a radical course of chemotherapy because it's such a shock to the body. It left me feeling sick and weak. While I was having chemotherapy I suffered blood clots in my arteries. It looked as though the cancer might not kill me but the treatment would. I kept telling myself that this was just a temporary setback. Each day I would focus on getting well and keeping a positive outlook. All things come to an end, I told myself. The drugs used in chemotherapy were now reacting in my body, making me feel drained and exhausted. As difficult as it was I decided to see it as an opportunity for a state of relaxed awareness, which I'd first learned about from Dr Ainslie Meares. Meditation had a wonderfully calming effect on me. It was quite magical, and it helped me become aware of my attitudes. I slowly began to transform the negative patterns I had been carrying for such a long time.

Three books that helped were Louise Hay's *You Can Heal Your Life*; *You Can Conquer Cancer* by Ian Gawler; and Dr Carl Simonton's *Getting Well Again*. I also learned about creative visualisation— imagining what you want, focusing on this and feeding what you're aiming for with lots of positive thoughts until it happens. So, I decided to use creative visualisation to see myself healed and well. Creative visualisation is a powerful healing tool.

When you visualise things as you'd like them to be, you attract those new things or outlook into your life.

These amazing new approaches made me even more determined to explore other holistic therapies. My sister-in-law was a great help. She and I wrote a list of possible alternative approaches that seemed well worth trying. I also wrote down my short- and long-term goals, including attending my son's graduation from university. I just knew I had to have things to work towards and look forward to.

As time went on I realised how important it was to avoid being negative. I asked the district nurses who visited me at home to talk only about positive things. I didn't want to hear about people who'd had a difficult time with cancer or who were dying. I wanted to focus only on living and getting well.

I also asked my family and friends to help. To my surprise, my request offended a few people. But when I stepped back I began to see how we make a habit of dwelling on other people's misfortunes by continually talking about how sad and difficult things are, instead of thinking about ways of helping. Idle gossip and pre-conceived judgments about others are negative and self-destructive. I didn't want to dwell on my situation or keep talking about it. I wanted time-out to reflect inwardly, to be still so that the answers I was seeking would reveal themselves.

During this time I had a number of beautiful radiance technique treatments, also known as reiki, which is the gentle laying on of hands. The practitioner simply channels the universal life-energy (which some people refer to as prana) into the body for healing. The sessions were non-invasive and nurturing, and they completely relaxed my body. They were so lovely. I didn't have to have a conversation. I didn't have to take off my clothes. Basically, I didn't have to participate—I could just be there and relax.

Although I didn't have much energy during my chemotherapy I began to go walking, just as I'd visualised. At first I couldn't walk very far, but distance wasn't the point. I kept on imagining myself walking strongly. I also practised saying 'No' whenever I could to the things I didn't want to do. I'd always felt a burden of responsibility in my relationships and I was tired, tired of compromising myself and my needs for others. This area in my life needed to change.

I started doing what I'd wanted to do for some time, simple things like listening to music or going to the movies. I went to the ballet, the theatre and attended some live concerts. Life was bright, vibrant and interesting, something I hadn't experienced for many years. I began to feel good about nurturing myself. I had vitamin C injections, herbal medicine and vitamin supplements, mistletoe injections for my tumours, colonic irrigations to clear my digestive tract, acupuncture to settle me, and aromatherapy.

But the most important therapy was learning to change my thoughts, attitudes and beliefs. My mother had given me a great gift because I saw what happened when you don't face up to your life and change.

She taught me that we are all conditioned to believe certain things and to behave in certain ways, and that this positive or negative conditioning can be passed on in families from one generation to the next. Without even realising it, we keep the same old patterns running over and over, causing us so much hurt and suffering.

The miracle is that healing is never just about us. Once we break our old patterns a whole new way of living can emerge.

When we heal ourselves, we literally help to heal the lives of those who come after us, because then the chains of the past have been forever broken.

<h1 style="text-align:center">3</h1>

A life-changing experience

Chemotherapy was challenging, but in the middle of my treatment something wonderful happened that turned my life around. One day while I was recovering from my latest round of treatment, my sister-in-law visited me. Just before she left she handed me a tape that she had used to lift her spirits when she felt stressed.

That night I fell wearily into bed with the tape. What a sight I must have looked, with my hair falling out, an intravenous catheter to administer chemotherapy in my breast, and not to forget the two plastic ends that stuck out over the top of my nightdress. The white turban I wore to cover the few sprouts of hair on my head lay crooked and twisted on my forehead, over it were the largest black Mickey Mouse earphones you've ever seen. I was ready and wired for bed. I turned on the tape to hear the beautiful words, 'Lord, hear my prayer', repeated over and over for the entire sixty minutes of the tape. I found myself saying these words silently until finally I slipped into a deep, peaceful sleep.

At around 2.30 in the morning I began to stir. Something was happening that was beyond my wildest imaginings. I felt love so strong that I could almost reach out and touch it. It was inside me and all around me. *Oh!* I felt the energy in the room expanding and heating up.

My heart began to beat louder and louder, and yet the sound of it seemed muffled as this immense love continued to grow and expand, radiating out into the room.

It was so amazing I hardly dared open my eyes. For a moment I felt scared, but my fear was absorbed immediately into this love. The heat around my feet was so fierce that they began to burn. They felt as if they were resting on a heater. My physical body seemed to move upwards. *Was I starting to float above the bed?* It didn't matter. I remember melting into this overwhelming, expansive love. It was like falling in love for the first time, except a thousand times better.

Slowly I opened my eyes and saw that a golden glow lit up the entire room. And there in front of me was a vision of the Lord Jesus, clothed in his ancient robes. His healing hands were about six centimetres from my feet, causing the burning sensation. I thought about the Bible story of Jesus raising Lazarus from the dead and realised that this was what He was doing now, raising the spirit in me from the dead. I looked into His eyes, they radiated pure love, and I became mesmerised by them. Then he glided from my feet to the left side of my bed holding his hands about twelve centimetres from my chest where the cancer was. Time blurred. He could have been there for two or ten minutes. To me there seemed to be no time.

The energy was uplifting and so intense, I gently closed my eyes to absorb the heat radiating around my chest. Eventually I felt the energy slowly withdraw from the room, and when

I opened my eyes, He was gone. My husband was blissfully unaware of everything that had happened. I fell back into a peaceful sleep.

When I awoke I promised myself that if I survived this illness, I would spend the rest of my life learning about and working with this marvellous life-energy we all possess. Little did I realise then that my life as an energetic and spiritual healer had begun on that wonderful, wonderful night.

4

Meeting the angels

There were more special experiences to come that were perfectly timed for me. I like to think of them as golden threads woven into the tapestry of my life. They began with a Dr Simonton tape that led me closer to connecting with the angels. When you work with this tape you are asked to imagine a warrior image or laser beam destroying the cancer cells in your body. I had great difficulty finding an image to work with, and became more and more uncomfortable with the process. The next day, in sheer desperation, I prayed for help to guide me in my morning meditation.

I waited for what seemed like minutes for any images to appear. Then I felt the urge to open my eyes and look up above me to the left. There on the wall next to my bed were the two golden cherubim angels that had belonged to my mother. It was as if I was seeing them for the first time. Tears welled up inside as a strange peace flowed through my whole body. I had my image! I could work with the angels and visualise using

17

their draped loin cloths to cleanse the cancer from my body every day. The angels would be my immune system's spiritual warriors, tirelessly eliminating the abnormal cancer cells from my body.

It was only when I looked back that I realised my connection with angels had begun years before. As I stood at the left side of my mother's bed after she had passed away, I took down the golden angels that had hung for many years on the wall and packed them carefully away. When we finally moved into our house, I made a special point of asking Bob to fix the set of angels to the wall beside my bed to remind me of my mother. How was I to know that those little golden cherubs would spark a lifelong love of angels?

Every day as I meditated and worked with the angels, I found myself being filled with a gentle energy of unconditional love. As my images of the angels became clearer and more vivid, my body became lighter and lighter until I became a ball of white silvery light. I began to feel an inner strength that I hadn't known before. I called to Archangel Raphael, the angel of healing, to help me in my daily quest. I felt loved and supported on my journey towards survival.

Six months after the end of my conventional therapy, I had an even more intense vision of a huge, white angel. I was undergoing a small bowel series test, where a tube was put down my throat, through my stomach and into the upper section of my small intestine. This exploration is done with no muscle relaxants and is not a test for the faint of heart.

I was feeling very anxious about the result, and uncomfortable, so I decided to slip into meditation while I was lying on the examination table. I asked silently for help. From the moment the tube passed down my throat I began to gag. The amazing thing was that instead of panicking I felt a great urge to breathe slowly, focus, and go deep inside. To my great surprise I saw myself begin to fill with light, and then a warm glowing wave moved through me. I lay there entranced by this magnetic energy and overwhelming love. The noise of the machines, and doctors and nurses, blurred into the background. I felt my body beginning to float. When I opened my eyes, out of the corner of my left eye, I could see an amazingly large white, winged being, gently floating about a metre from my body. It was the shape of an angel. I closed my eyes again and melted into the warmth and love, only to be brought back into the room by the doctor calling me, and asking me if I was okay. I can still remember his words as he rolled me over onto my back and quickly pulled the tube from deep within my intestine.

'How did you do that?' he said.

'What?' I asked.

'What were you doing?'

'Nothing,' I replied.

He then told me that in all the years he had been administering this particular test it had taken him between seven to fifteen times to get the tube down a patient's throat. In my case it took only once. I smiled gently at him, grateful for the angel who had helped me through this difficult process, and who let me know that in life we never truly walk alone.

It's many years since that experience, but I continue to work with my angels and guides. These days I love to help others connect with their angels, because there is no situation that is too small or difficult for them. They are there for all of us.

5
A leap of faith

So much has happened it's hard to believe I was once such a sad, stressed-out person. I loved how I felt so much, that I read everything I could get my hands on about energy and healing. Then one morning a girlfriend dropped in to see me with a prospectus for a course about the ancient wisdom teachings. She was going to enrol and asked me to join her, so I did.

I began studying courses in spiritual healing and personal growth. I ended up studying for nine years. *Whew!* It was a lot of work, but worth it, because I was doing what I felt passionately about. I even won an award for best clinical skills in energetic healing at the college, and was invited to teach there. All this study wasn't easy because my long-held beliefs, including those from my Catholic upbringing, were often confronted. As a child I loved being in the chapel and hearing the nuns sing, and when I was about nine, I saw this huge white light glowing in front of me. I never told anyone about this special moment and it has remained with me.

However, when I look back, I realise I associated God with fear, control, pain, guilt and suffering. Was I such a bad person? I clearly remember the hot summer's morning when I was nineteen and I decided to stop going to church. Twenty years later, when I was diagnosed with cancer, I realised that in cutting my ties with the church I had also become separated from my inner spirit.

When I was very ill with cancer I contacted someone involved in a Christian group. When they visited the house they'd read a short excerpt from the Bible, pray, and then someone would talk in a language I was not familiar with. It was described as talking in tongues. I now understand that this woman was channelling the essence of spirit, which is what an energetic or spiritual healer does without talking in tongues.

The first time one of the people in the group put her hand on my shoulder I was blown away. I saw a massive ball of light, the same as the one I'd seen when I was nine years old and was drawn into its centre. It was like an out-of-body experience: I lost all awareness of my physical body as my energy merged into the light. There was no sense of time or space. The experience was enormously uplifting, and the lightness stayed with me for days. Yet, while I got a lot of help from the group, I wanted to discover more about the energy I was feeling.

Then, one day I was talking with a doctor from Sri Lanka who had studied in a monastery for years. He was writing a book about life and spirituality, and sensed my distress at choosing from the varied pathways spirituality can take. 'Annie, Annie,' he said gently, 'It is all one. It is all the same.' In that moment my anguish melted away, and tears rolled down my cheeks. I was deeply moved to realise that there are hundreds and hundreds of ways life speaks to us.

I felt at that moment I was on my way home. It's a wonderful feeling—I've had it many times since. It is always a great indicator that I am on the right track. I now know that God, the Universe, heals and that healers such as those I experienced in that group are simply instruments for healing. By the power of their intention, prayer, and connection with the Holy Spirit, they direct this energy through their hands to the patient. This was a powerful lesson for me and another step towards understanding the mystical experiences we all have.

6

Starting to heal

*T*he wonderful thing is that *everyone* can do what I do. You just have to be open, and trust what you feel and see. Some people are aware of these gifts from an early age, but for others, like myself, it takes particular life experiences to reconnect with them.

During my studies I learned to understand a whole lot more of what I was seeing and feeling. Over time I developed a kind of personal dictionary of signs and symbols to explain what I saw and felt. (For instance, the presence of a golden light around a person tells me that they have done some soul work.) This wonderful language of symbols varies from one person to another—you might see someone who has done soul work quite differently, though the message is the same.

You might not think you're able to pick up these kind of details about the people and places around you, yet you've probably picked up on someone's vibes at some stage. You might have met a complete stranger and known immediately that you would be long-term friends, or felt you already knew all about them. Or perhaps you've been somewhere new and have had a sense of déjà vu about the place, even though you've never laid eyes on it before. These and other experiences show that you have the ability to feel and see beyond the obvious.

It took me a while to trust in my intuition and it didn't happen until I studied reiki and learned to lay my hands on someone and act as a channel for the healing life-energy to enter their body.

When we work with others, respect for their free will is very important. Before we start any healing work we must ask a person's permission to tap into their energy and access information that might be useful for the session. In asking permission, you are honouring the person's right to privacy and the integrity of their soul (because we don't know what a person's soul path should be). I was told by my reiki teacher to ask three times to be sure, by saying the client's name aloud or silently, then awaiting the inner response before beginning the session.

If someone comes for a healing session, then it is understood that they are giving permission. But in the case of absent healing, where you are not working face-to-face with that person, it is important to ask for permission.

In the early days, when I was learning how to work with energy, I decided to send some energy to a male relative. I was sure I'd get a quick and easy 'Yes'. During the class, as we all sat to send healing energy to someone, I looked lovingly at the photo of this relative, tuned in, and asked him by name if he wanted absent healing. The first thought that came to me was 'No'. I quickly dismissed the response, thinking I hadn't done it correctly.

I tried again. And again I got a 'No'. *Hmmm!* I looked around to see all the other students beginning their treatment and felt a little silly, so I tried again, and this time I sensed an even more decisive 'No'. I quietly asked the reiki teacher for help, and she suggested I try someone else. As I took a different photo from my bag, she asked if she could take my relative's photo and ask for permission to heal.

I began on another person, tuning in and asking for permission. The answer was a clear 'Yes'. *Phew!* Later the reiki teacher told me that my relative had also clearly said 'No' to her. It happens from time to time because sometimes people are not ready to receive this type of healing energy. It was a powerful lesson not to doubt the answer you receive when you ask. You may not understand why you receive the answer, but that's not the point. You have to respect a person's integrity and their right to choose if or when they want healing.

Once you start trusting your senses, you find that other kinds of information start to come to you.

Sometimes I have information down-loaded about something when I'm thinking about something entirely different. I was on a plane to Belgium and there was a young woman sitting a couple of seats ahead of me. For hours I read and dozed, then got up for some exercise. As I walked past her, a whole lot of information came to me about that young woman, including an issue she was struggling with at that time. When I turned back, I noticed she was reading an astrology book, and plucked up the courage to comment on it. The seat next to her was available, so I sat down and we talked like long-lost friends. In those few seconds she bared her soul, and I gave her all the information that had come to me.

Afterwards, she thanked me warmly. 'What you told me was exactly what I needed to know right now,' she said. 'It will help me make some very big decisions.' This often happens to me. The interesting thing is that afterwards I don't remember any of it.

The magical thing is that we can all do the same thing. We can serve each other by passing on important information that comes to us in this way. This is not about trying to control another person or show off. It has nothing to do with our ego. The information comes *through* you, but it is not *of* you. When it happens, you know what you have to do. It takes practice, care and love to help others in this way, and it is so rewarding, because none of us was meant to be an island.

Get in touch with your wisdom

Try this exercise to help you reconnect with your body's wisdom by focusing on your feelings.

Find a place where you won't be disturbed and make yourself comfortable. Close your eyes and sit quietly for a few moments. Now, recall a joyful experience in your life. It might have been when you received some good news or when you were at a great celebration or were with a person you loved deeply.

Keep that experience in mind as you remember where it took place. Notice where you were when it happened and who was with you. Did it happen when you were a child, an adolescent, a young adult or later?

Notice also how you were standing at the time and how you were feeling. Were you standing tall or sitting? Were you animated? Were you feeling cocooned from the world? Exactly where in your body did you feel this joy? Now, change the joy to sadness and repeat the exercise.

By practising this exercise regularly, you will start to recognise where you experience feelings in your body. This will help you understand the signals your body gives you at different times.

7
Reading energy

As I progressed in my studies I came to appreciate just how wonderful our bodies are, and that we are a whole lot more than flesh and blood. Once a real sceptic, I now know that everything that lives—people, animals, trees, plants—has an aura, also known as an energy field.

Over the years, as I took the time to silence my mind and trust my experiences, I began to see the auras we have, which surround and pass through our physical body. They look just like the light around the flame of a candle. In healthy people the aura shows up as a flow of bright colours. Unhealthy people have dark patches in their aura. When there is darkness around any of the areas of the body, I find there is a strong blockage in the aura. Basically, the flow of energy has been stopped and over time it can become hardened like a crystal. Where the patches of stuck energy appear can be a warning site for developing illness.

Whenever a client is coming for a session, I read their aura clairvoyantly beforehand. Later, during the session, a client might tell me about their broken leg, arm or collarbone, and to their surprise these injuries correspond with what I've already picked up on in their energy field. Before Sarah came for a session, I found darkness in her energy field around her right forearm. She told me later that she'd broken her wrist twice before she was fifteen.

When Brad came to see me, I saw a crystallised blockage around his throat. This area was very dark, as though it had become solid. Clients with throat blockages are always trying to clear their throat, have a faint voice, or trouble with their throat in some way. Throat issues can relate to an inability to speak out at home, work or in family situations. Or it may be due to relationship difficulties, where you never feel heard. It's like your communication has been stifled.

Just as you may have scar tissue after an operation, so you can have energy scarring or imprints in your aura. I have the ability to see these imprints in a person's aura. Would you believe that even the chemicals from an anaesthetic can get trapped in your cells and aura? At one stage, after my major health issues, I was in a deep healing meditation when something amazing happened. I was suddenly overwhelmed by the smell of anaesthetic. It was then I realised I had been carrying this energy in my cells and aura for sixteen years. When I came out of the healing I felt so much lighter, as though I had had an inner and outer spring clean.

Sometimes I see cords in a person's aura. We all have connections with people, places or things we come into contact with. Some connections are positive, others are not. If we form an unhealthy attachment with someone we literally plug into them; it's like an electric cord between two people. As healers, we call this cording. These cords look like threads. They can be thick, limp, dense, old, dark or faint. Cords form in children with overly protective and possessive parents. They also form in relationships where someone has become infatuated with a person. Anywhere there is an obsessive, unhealthy attachment to someone else, you can be sure there's some cording going on. You might like to think about your relationships for a minute. Where might there be some cording happening?

How to cut cords

Sit in a quiet place and gently close your eyes. Begin to think of the person you need to cut the cord with. See this person covered in a violet veil for protection, and try to see the areas (there could be more than one) where you appear to be corded. Then say the following words to free up the energy flowing between you. 'I forgive you, I forgive myself. I pray for your prospering where ever you may go. I release you now in love and light.' As you say the last sentence, visualise yourself using a pair of golden scissors to cut the cord. Wait for a few seconds then allow any images to fade away into the distance. Finish the process by surrounding yourself in a bubble of white or pink light. It may be helpful to repeat this process a few times.

8

That heavy feeling

There are many ways I see energy in a person's aura. Some people have a heaviness around them that often looks like a dense, dark cloud and may encompass a part or the whole of the body.

Myra had trouble settling in class. She was agitated and couldn't concentrate on anything for more than a minute. As I focused my attention around her head, Myra had what looked like a blob of a black sticky substance suspended in her aura. At that time I was confused by what I was seeing. However, months later, when I ran into her unexpectedly out of town, she shared her difficulties with drug addiction. She said it felt like she was going mad. Her addiction stopped her from being coordinated, attentive and focused in her life. Though Myra initially thought taking drugs was a great escape, she came to realise they took away her ability to support herself and be positive, focused and constructive. When a person has used a lot of drugs, to an energetic healer it feels like we're moving our hands through treacle. This is the result of built-up toxicity in the aura.

If there is a lot of heaviness in and around a person's head, this could suggest depression or that the person has had some type of trauma or operation to this area. They could be struggling with ongoing negative thought patterns that are driving them to distraction or, in some cases, destruction.

At times the challenges and responsibilities of life can feel as if we're pulling a heavy chain or carrying the world on our shoulders. This is the same with your aura. Even though it's invisible to the naked eye, your aura can *feel* heavy, full and dark. When a practitioner slowly rakes the aura with their outstretched hands, in the same motion as you would rake the ground, and feels a dragging sensation, it is an indication there's built-up heavy energy. Raking your aura is just like combing your hair using your fingers. When you do this it's like opening up the doors and windows of your house to let in the sunshine. Basically, you are opening your aura to receive more light.

Heaviness in someone's aura can also indicate that another person has latched on to them and is drawing on their personal energy. It may be a needy friend, a relative, co-worker or a demanding partner.

Elise didn't realise how sensitive she was. After returning from a holiday and settling back at work, she found herself quickly feeling angry and resentful. Her body was showing signs of discomfort around the back of the neck and shoulders. She felt tired and drained. As she talked, I was able to pick up the silhouette of three women in her aura. It turned out the heaviness Elise had connected to was the overload of thoughts and emotions from her work colleagues. I suggested before she went to bed to clear her personal energy and cut the cords to the people she'd identified to me as described in Chapter 7. She reported feeling lighter, more energised and pain-free the next morning.

9

Feeling toxic

If we pay attention there's so much our bodies and our auras can reveal. When I'm assessing someone's aura, I become aware of any distortions in the flow of the energy. Energy appears in many different forms. Sometimes I see dragging in the aura. The words that come to me, like the symbols I mentioned earlier, paint a picture of the irregular and distorted patterns that clients are dealing with. As I describe what I have picked up on, it helps them re-connect to the feelings associated with past events, traumas, accidents, physical discomforts or illnesses. These links reflect memories of the pain that is stored in their cells. When clients come, and I share with them my impressions, they are quickly able to recognise their physical, mental and emotional issues—their patterns of pain.

When I pick up what looks like a yellow-brownish fluid, like an oil slick, in someone's energy field it indicates that this person's aura has become a dumping ground, like a rubbish tip. Just as your skin can absorb air particles, so can your aura. We can also absorb or be sensitive to chemicals and toxic metals. Even your own toxic thoughts, and those of people around you, can create toxicity in your aura. Ingesting or breathing toxic material from the environment where you live, work or play can affect your energy levels. This could be a bullying boss, a difficult work colleague or an aggressive, controlling or punishing partner. It could be those friends and family who constantly dump their stressful life situations on you. Toxicity in your aura can also be caused by heavy smoking and excessive alcohol consumption. Poor digestion can show up in the aura around the stomach as toxic energy. Chemotherapy and radiotherapy can also leave a yellow-brown or black toxicity in the aura.

When I first started to work as a dental nurse I was exposed to considerable amounts of radiation when I took x-rays. I also worked with amalgam, which is partly made up of mercury. The radiation and mercury was then absorbed into my body through the skin, and into my aura. Over time this compromised my immune system. I wonder what my aura would have looked like then, as illness always shows up in the aura first.

Whatever we can't stomach—whether it's a thought, a situation or place you find yourself in—can create toxicity. What makes you feel sick to the stomach can literally show up in your aura. So, if someone has experienced abuse—emotionally, mentally or physically—wherever they experienced this abuse in their body is mirrored in their aura. This area of their aura may have contracted, withered or withdrawn. When a person feels the need to protect themselves in some way, let's say because of fear, their aura will contract inwards, as though trying to lock or hide that part of them away from harm.

When there has been an overcompensation of energy to one side of an aura and body, this gives me further clues to what is going on. If a person has a more dominant left-hand side it could indicate they are comfortable with the feeling, receptive female side of themselves, but are not necessarily able to assert themselves, to use the strong masculine part of who they are. Your masculine, assertive self is on your right-hand side. To be healthy we need a balance of both male and female energies in our aura. Where do you tend to have aches and pains? On your left- or right-hand side of your body?

When there's a sense of dragging in your energy field, the aura can look like a stretched out cloud on a windy day. This gives me the sense the person is being pulled in one direction, or their thoughts are focused in an obsessive way. The side on which the dragging appears, whether left or right, is also significant. I then look for where the dragging occurs in relation to the body. The direction of the dragging tells me if it's associated with a male or female figure, like a strong mother or father, and which environment it relates to.

10
Shrinking violets

Gina, who was in her fifties, contacted me after a friend suggested energetic healing might help her. Before Gina arrived, I sat quietly, centred myself then tuned in to her energy. As with all my clients, I look to see what is happening around their head area first. This is to determine if they have a connection to their inner spirit or divinity. If this is the case I'll see some type of symbolic golden light.

There was a golden cord from the top of Gina's head leading upwards, but it was darkened. I sensed that past experiences had made her fearful about connecting fully to her divine self. I also saw golden energy pouring down from around her head. Her head energy appeared flat, as though there was no vitality there, and stopped at her heart. This told me she had closed herself off from receiving the beautiful golden light in her life, which left her feeling temporarily disconnected and confused. By not trusting her divine self she was experiencing a loss of energy, as our life-energy is a divine gift. Basically, Gina had a sense of emptiness and loss of faith in herself.

Gina's life-energy was withdrawn on the left side of her aura. The left side is significant because it is associated with the maternal side of our family. I picked up that Gina's mother had been a powerful influence in her life, but that Gina had not always been in harmony with her. There was a contraction of energy on this side of her body, as though she was protecting herself from something.

I see this shrinking away of a person's aura quite a lot and it happens when we try to protect ourselves from painful people and situations. Sometimes there is a shrinking of the aura, either on the left- or right-hand side, in to the physical body. Contraction can appear around the energy centres (chakras) and the many layers of the aura. This can signify an accident, illness, fear, excessive worry or lack of connection to feelings.

When I saw Keith, I sensed that his energy was very much drawn towards the right side of his body. Again this was an important piece of information because the right side is associated with the father's side of the family. As I tuned in more closely this told me something was going on in Keith's relationship with his father, or the way he saw himself as a man in the world.

So, when we feel like shrinking away from certain influences, this withdrawal shows up in the aura. If we don't deal with this, stepping back can become a habit, and people can start to see us as a doormat.

Change the thought

When we feel like a doormat we are coming from a place of fear and lack of empowerment. We are often playing the role of a victim to our past circumstances. We are stuck in a familiar pattern. Try and remember that at the circumference of our fear is freedom and light. Give yourself permission to feel the fear so that you can experience what is beyond it. One small step is all it takes. Change the thought and change your mind. Use some affirmations like 'I now love and approve of myself', 'I now take charge of my life', 'I am a powerful person.'

11
No secrets

The more we get to understand the intricacies of a person's aura, the more they can reveal. Laura called one morning, desperate for help. As I tuned into her life-energy before she arrived, I found that it was moving in an upward direction, from her feet to her head. This told me she was having difficulty being grounded in her life. This upward movement, or sweeping of life-energy, generally tells me the person's overwhelmed by their thoughts and emotions. This causes them to be very unsettled and ungrounded. In Laura's case, a recent shock and personal realisation had literally swept her off her feet.

Laura had suddenly been confronted with a life situation that wasn't fitting in with what she had envisioned for herself. She had reached a certain age and time in her life where she had hoped to be married and possibly starting a family. There was a great sense of grief and loss. Laura could see no immediate resolution in her situation.

This sweeping movement of life-energy can also happen in reverse, to any part of your energy fields. The sweeping upwards or downwards in the aura happens when there is fast and furious change or shock in your life, causing you to feel as if you've left part of yourself behind. This can also happen when things have come to a standstill. The energy of the aura builds up on one side causing stagnation. For Laura, it was the realisation that she was stuck, lacking change or direction. Being suddenly confronted with this was, quite naturally, overwhelming for her.

There was a lot of light coming from around the sides of Laura's head, but what looked like a grey-coloured substance spilled over her forehead, covering her third eye—the area between the eyebrows. The third eye is where you perceive truth, what is real and unreal.

Laura had strong thoughts that were confusing her and she felt heavy headed. She also felt she was becoming irrational, and feared losing control. This fear was affecting her current relationship and her trust in herself and others. Still, I could see from the light around the sides of her head that Laura had some connection to her own inner spirit. She'd certainly done some work on herself, which always helps—because connection to your spirit brings balance. Even if you've lost your balance, you know what it feels like to be whole.

I also found that there was a series of cuts across Laura's throat, suggesting that her head and heart were disconnected. I sensed that Laura tended to live in her head and not connect with her feelings or the rest of her body. We do this when we're finding that life's too painful. It's a coping mechanism.

I often see a cutting off around the throat and reproductive area, but it can happen anywhere in the body. It tells me that the person has in some way disconnected from their inner knowing, creating blocked feelings and miscommunication with themselves and others.

The energy around Laura's heart was darkened. This doesn't mean that she's a bad person. As I felt my way into her heart area energetically, I found there was a great deal of sadness about unresolved relationships. If they'd been resolved they wouldn't show up as darkness around the heart. When I see darkness in a person's aura this is similar to when I see heaviness. It suggests the person has experienced trauma, disease, fear, guilt or abuse. It can also indicate that the client knew a person who has died, but still holds a strong emotional attachment for them.

As well, Laura appeared to be carrying a heavy backpack out of which streamed brown, gooey toxic water. It looked as though someone had split the backpack to allow this toxic water to flow out. Water is associated with emotions, for Laura these toxic emotions were streaming out behind her back. This suggested to me that there were painful things that Laura kept from view, even from herself.

I noticed too that Laura's aura was a cylinder shape instead of the normal healthy egg shape. There was a strong sense that Laura felt contained in her life, being pressured from both left and right. This told me that I needed to explore her relationship with her mum (left side) and dad (right side), because this pressure was literally impacting on her whole energy field.

Feel the enegy in your body

Over the next few days, notice where you connect with the energy in your body during encounters with others. For example, if a colleague talks to you aggressively, notice where you feel the energy in your body. When someone talks to you with respect and care, notice where you feel the energy in your body. When you are feeling pressured by someone else's demands, notice where you feel the energy in your body.

By practising this exercise, you will gradually raise your awareness about your own energy field and the energy fields of people around you.

12

You are a magnet

All energy is magnetic by nature, attracting to itself more of itself. Your thoughts are like your own personal magnets. A positive outlook attracts positive outcomes.

When things seem to be going wrong in your life, it often seems that you can't get out of the negative spiral. Bills need to be paid, you become ill, your relationships are difficult, and you feel that things just won't get better. You ask yourself, 'What did I do to deserve this?' or you say, 'It isn't fair. Other people don't seem to have these worries.' But according to the law of attraction, your thoughts have *attracted* this situation. If your thoughts focus on what is not working in your life, then you'll find that more of what is not working is attracted to you. And so it goes.

In the same way, when you focus on good things, when you feel grateful for what you have, when you can laugh things off and don't take life too seriously, you find that life continues to be good. You seem to have what people call lucky breaks.

What is actually happening is that you are attracting all this good fortune and synchronicity because of your thoughts. It can be difficult to accept that you attract some things into your life. How can it possibly be? How could you really decide to attract painful, negative circumstances, for example? Well, it's hard to swallow, but that's how it works.

If you can pinpoint what it is you are thinking about and creating for yourself, then you can change it. Your life today is the product of your life in the past. All those thoughts and attitudes you've had until now have brought you to where you are today. Think about that.

This means that you *can* create a new reality for yourself. You can attract health, love, happiness and enjoy a wonderful sense of wellbeing. You can have fulfilling relationships and a satisfying career. It's a matter of attending to your thoughts.

Everything and everyone you attract to you becomes in some way a reflection or mirror image of yourself.

When I wanted to heal from cancer, I made sure that I had positive thoughts and I surrounded myself only with positive energy. I didn't want to hear about people who hadn't survived cancer or other illness. I didn't want to hear about despair, depression or helplessness. I didn't want to hear about people who were struggling with sickness. It was hard for some people around me to stick to this approach, but it was essential for me to heal.

I wanted to hear uplifting stories about how people survived and helped to heal themselves. I wanted to focus on how good life is, and hear how all things are possible! I knew that those positive thoughts would radiate out and attract good health and wellbeing. My sense of humour was as strong as ever, and was a great gift. Actually, it is a gift for everyone to be able to laugh or giggle at some of the silly little things that happen. When I was intent on healing, I laughed and giggled a lot.

Mind you, I'd learned to do all this after years of not understanding why I was miserable. It took a serious illness—in fact, a series of serious illnesses—for me to realise that I was attracting it all to me. I was keeping the old familiar patterns going, thinking the same negative things, and feeling the same old negative feelings.

It always happens at a subconscious level. This is where you need to raise your awareness.

I'm not saying it's wrong to feel grief, anger or sadness. They are natural human emotions that can be used as a catalyst to transform your life. It's only when you allow yourself to wallow, when you keep telling other people how bad you feel and how terrible life is and how things will keep on being bad, and so on, that it's unhealthy. Remember, according to the law of attraction, if you think like that you'll keep attracting the same old horrible stuff.

When Georgia came to see me she was frustrated at work and wanted something to change. As she talked her attitude to herself and those around her was painfully obvious.

'It's like it was at school,' she said. 'The same old thing except everybody's a bit older. There's a group of women who gang up on me. When I walk past them, I'm sure they look me up and down and laugh behind my back. They're really nasty types. The trouble is, the same thing happened at my last job. I can't seem to get away from these kinds of people.'

There are various threads to Georgia's story, but for now we'll look at the aspect of attraction. It was clear to me that Georgia's thoughts were causing her life to be miserable. Wherever she went she expected people to shun her and to laugh at her. She expected people, and women in particular, to be 'really nasty types'. And guess what? Everywhere she went she found really nasty types. They were drawn to her, exactly like magnets, because she was attracting the very thing she thought about and expected to happen. Funny about that!

One of the things I worked on with Georgia was to change her way of thinking. And to do this I passed on to her the tool of creative visualisation. Each morning, before leaving the house, she actively imagined enjoying herself at work, interacting happily with the others, joining in the fun. She kept on seeing herself getting on with everyone she met and worked with.

Your emotions are keys to your inner self, revealing your responses to life's circumstances.

And again, guess what? Yes, it wasn't long before Georgia noticed a change in the people around her. She was now vibrating at a higher level and she was attracting only those who met that same positive vibe. People who harboured nasty thoughts and attitudes just kept away. Georgia drew to her those who vibrated at the same frequency, which was now much higher than before.

13

Your personal space

When I began my studies into how our bodies work, a whole new world began to open up. It often felt like I was seeing the world around me for the very first time. I was aware that everyone had an aura, but I'd no idea how much information auras revealed about us. Whenever anyone refers to someone's aura we tend to think they're going all psychic on us, because they don't realise that auras are made up of electromagnetic energy. It was exciting to discover just how much our auras can tell about how we're tracking in life—whether we're feeling worried or critical of ourselves, constantly angry or depressed, and so on. Because our lives change all the time, so too do our auras. Once you know how, you can see someone's long-term issues in their aura, as well as things that are happening for them right now.

Even though you may not be able to read auras, you often pick up on the vibes you get from someone's aura. It doesn't seem to matter whether it's a person you know well or a

48

complete stranger. Often we can sense a person's unspoken resentment, their quiet despair or lack of self-confidence, and so on. The same is true when you behave lovingly or in a hateful way—it can be seen in your aura. Often you can feel what another person is feeling. This can also be the case when someone touches you, or brushes past you. Sometimes it's a pleasant experience. At other times it may make your flesh crawl. Without realising it, you're picking up on what is going on for that person. Basically, you're reading what they're carrying around in their aura or energy field.

The more I got to know about auras, the more I began to realise that in some ways our whole lives are reflected in our auras. It's this information that psychic people tap into when they give a reading. The information in our auras also helps practitioners get a handle on how life is for you at present. They can do this because they have been trained to tune into a person's aura and see what's going on. They can sense where you're on top of things, where your weak spots are, and where you may be overstretching yourself. They can sense, feel and see what parts of you are out of balance.

When life wasn't as busy, many more people were able to read auras without having to learn how. Often small children can see auras without any effort, because they're more in tune with life, and not so busy or distracted. However, once they get into TV and computers and all the other things that take up their time, sadly they tend to lose these abilities. The wonderful thing is that with practice anyone can learn to see and read auras. Technology enables us to benefit from Kirlian photography. You can now have a photo taken of your aura, and then have someone knowledgeable interpret the information. The whole point of reading auras is to gain a better sense of how you are moving through life. Your aura can literally mirror where you are in the present moment.

Every subtle layer of your aura has a job to do. When each layer of your aura is in balance, then you're in good shape physically, mentally, emotionally and spiritually. It's not hard to know when you are in balance, because everything in life seems to flow to you in the right timing. Good ideas and positive people move in your pathway without effort. You get through everything you have to do without exhausting yourself. All this is possible because your life-energy can flow effortlessly through your aura and into your physical body. Your aura simply becomes more magnetic.

As you learn about all the different parts of the aura, you begin to appreciate just how intricate we are. So, what about our auras? Shortly we'll take a look in more depth at each layer, but just to give you some idea of what is going on in your aura, here's a sneak preview. You may like to look at Figure 1, The subtle layers of your aura, as you read on so you start to become more familiar with your aura. Don't worry if you can't take it all in, as we'll be going into more detail shortly. If you look at the diagram you can see the different layers of your aura. Each layer has its own job to do. The different layers govern the mental, emotional and spiritual parts of who you are.

The first three layers of your aura relate to your everyday life and to the world around you. Starting from your physical body, you can get a sense of each layer.

❀ Your etheric body supplies the life-energy to your body.
❀ Your astral body governs your passions and emotions. It's the part of us that leaves our physical body during out-of-body experiences.

Figure 1: The subtle layers of your aura

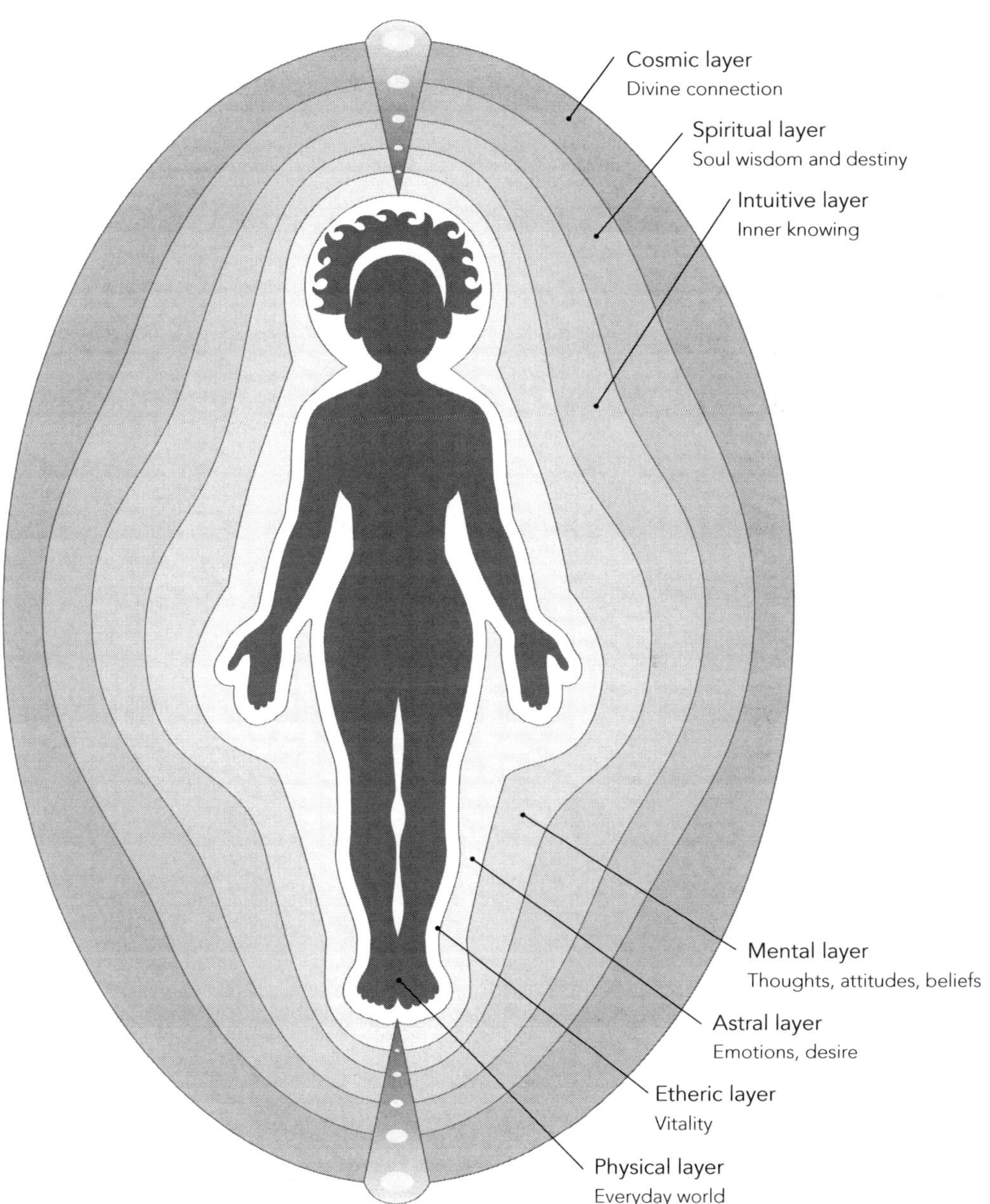

❀ Your mental body reflects your thoughts and beliefs.

From here you move to the more *spiritual* aspects of who you are.

❀ Your intuitive body is connected to your inner knowing, your intuition.
❀ Your spiritual body is linked to your spiritual wellbeing and destiny.
❀ Your cosmic body is connected to your divine self.

The great news is that with a bit of practice everyone can see auras. Once you start to see auras, you may begin to see a brilliant palette of colours and textures moving in and out of the aura. These colours help reveal how someone is feeling. While this may all be new to you, as it was for me, when you start to learn about what the colours mean, you begin to realise that many of our everyday expressions refer to what the different colours mean. We're all very familiar with such expressions as 'seeing red', 'feeling blue' or 'green with envy', describing how we might feel at times. Phrases such as 'the scent of fear' hint also at the idea that people could sense these aspects of the aura in the past. The fact we use these expressions when referring to people's emotions, suggests that our ancestors could read auras. We'll look at colours in a bit more depth shortly.

So, what else does your aura reveal? What we now know is that blockages or gaps in a person's aura help us see where illnesses are likely to appear in the physical body further down the track. So, by tuning into someone's aura, seeing an imbalance and healing it, we can help prevent more serious illnesses later on. Basically, your aura can be a wonderful early-warning system, if you take note of it. There are many ways we can pick up on these imbalances. Seeing muddy colours in someone's aura hints that something needs balancing. Those who are very sensitive are also able to pick up discordant sounds, or unpleasant flavours and smells in a person's aura, which again indicate the presence of some form of imbalance or illness.

As well as reflecting what's going on inside you, your aura reacts to what's going on in your immediate environment. So, if you're living in a toxic relationship, spending time in a confrontational workplace, or dealing with major life issues in the family or with close friends, these influences will also affect the health of your aura, which will in turn affect your physical body.

It's not just stuff that's happening for you right now that gets stored in your aura. Past hurts and traumas, unless dealt with, get stored there as well. These imbalances can impact on your life in all kinds of ways. They're one of the reasons we keep repeating unhelpful patterns, why we have the same kneejerk reactions to certain people or situations, and why we suffer recurrent health problems.

All this boils down to the fact that everything in the universe is made up of energy. You too are made of energy, moving particles that interact with each other. Sometimes these interactions are strained or hurtful. Sometimes they're joyous and inspiring. It just depends on what sort of energy you're carrying around with you in your aura.

The size of your aura also depends on how you're tracking. If you have little self-worth or are fearful, then the layers of your aura contract, giving you a greater sense of protection. If you're a confident person, or someone with a big personality, you've a sizeable aura to match. No-one's aura is static, however. When a timid person feels at home somewhere their aura is likely to open up a bit as they come out of their shell. And when a confident person is out of their depth, their aura is likely to contract. So, there's a lot going on in your aura. The more you know about auras, the more insight you have into yourself and others.

14

Your personal powerhouse

Having looked at my experiences with energy, and how I interpret people's energy, let's now look at auras in more detail. They are divided into seven subtle layers or planes, which have a further seven layers or subplanes. Within their structure a lot of knowledge and information is stored.

So, what does an aura look like? Just as an egg is contained by its shell, your aura is held within what is called an auric egg. This egg-shaped shell has openings above your head and below your feet. These openings connect you to the divine and to the Earth. They are like doorways for incoming life-energy that enable you to do everything you do.

Your spleen also draws in this life-energy. It then filters, sorts and distributes this life-energy through 72,000 pathways around your entire body. These remarkable pathways or threads of light are also known as nadis. They are woven together into a gossamer-thin tapestry, which brings together the physical and non-physical parts of yourself into one beautiful whole. The nadis network is like a carbon copy of your nervous system.

All life-energy comes from the sun. The incoming life-energy to the spleen chakra has some very important functions. It helps your blood and endocrine, nervous and immune systems function properly. Basically, it's what makes you an energetic, positive person.

Every breath you take circulates, maintains and transforms the life-energy in and around your body so that you can be healthy and vibrant. This breath also vitalises every layer of your aura.

Your aura is constantly changing, pulsing with life and exchanging energy with your physical body. Each layer of your aura *vibrates* at a different rate. The closer they are to your physical body, the slower the rate of vibration. This is due, in part, to the slower, denser nature of the Earth energies. To survive and thrive, your body needs to work well in the Earth's atmosphere. The further they move out from the body, the faster, finer and lighter the vibration is.

Our life-force energy is a 'sea' of pulsating centers, fields and pathways.' Julie Collett

For most people this wonderful dance of life-energy tends to remain unseen to the naked eye. However, you still connect with your own, or someone else's, aura on a day-to-day basis. One of the easiest ways to identify just how different people's energy can be is by sensing and feeling it. I bet you have had the experience of meeting someone for the first time and it just didn't feel right, even to the point of being really uncomfortable. When this person stepped closer to you,

you might have found yourself stepping back, not wanting them in your personal space. When this happens you have connected to another person's energy field.

Perhaps you have had the opposite reaction and the person's energy felt really comfortable, compatible to your own. Even though you had never set eyes on this person before it was as though you were meeting a long-lost friend. This is a good and positive example of meeting another person's energy field.

Let's say you are checking out a home to live in, and as you walk around the property you get a feeling or a vibe about it. It could be a positive or negative vibe. What's happening is your aura is picking up on the energy of the home and its surroundings. It's as though your energy sends out feelers and is picking up on what does or doesn't feel right for you. Then, like a bio-feedback system, it sends you a signal telling you this house is okay or no, it's not okay. This is what our psychic senses are doing all the time. What is truly fascinating is that this process is usually unconscious on our part!

How we express ourselves is a result of the way we consciously or unconsciously use our energy!

Your energy impressions as relayed from your psychic senses are also being registered by major energy centres, the chakras, in your body. Your chakras are like mini CDs that store important information, just like you do on your computer. Like CDs in use, they are constantly spinning.

So how does this happen? If you're in the house and don't like the vibes, it's because your senses have already scanned the place, then matched the vibes you've picked up with your own past experiences. The feedback from these energy files are the yes/no thoughts we have as our response. Truly amazing! It's your solar plexus chakra that registers these vibes. That's why we often say, 'I just had a *gut feeling* that something wasn't right.'

The energy your spinning chakras draw in penetrates your physical body. And, located between the belly button and the sternum, at the same time it spins outward, penetrating all the subtle layers of your aura. This energy is electromagnetic, so if you're an angry person it will draw angry people and situations towards you. When we don't understand energy, life can be frustrating and confusing because we don't know why stuff keeps happening to us. Once we get how our life-energy works, we can finetune our intuitive senses and be much more aware of the vibes we put out, as well as those vibes that come back to us. Then we can make more informed decisions about what we do and how we interact with others.

Like electricity, we sense our life-energy, but can't see it. And, like electricity, life-energy flows through a whole network to reach us. In some people this energy supply can feel like there is a dimmer switch on, suppressing the amount of light and energy available. So, they have low energy levels and frequently feel tired. Those with an abundance of energy may only sense a disruption in their energy supply when they are sick or have overextended themselves by burning the candle at both ends.

15
Who are you really?

Our auras are more intricate than we give them credit for. The lower layers that are closest to the body are the easiest to see and feel. Every layer looks and feels different to an energetic healer or a sensitive clairvoyant due to its vibrational frequency. Heavy energy is denser. Each layer of your aura has a slightly different job to do. The first layer, the *etheric body*, is a sheer garment surrounding your physical body. It looks like a transparent double of your physical body and extends 2–6 centimetres out from your skin.

Your etheric body looks like an intricate web, and can range in colour from light blue to grey. Because the etheric body is associated with the element fire, it can also glow like a golden light. When a person becomes enlightened it is the glow of this light that is seen around their head. It is commonly seen in Christian paintings as a halo around saints and angels denoting their spiritual illumination.

The etheric body holds the blueprint of your destiny in this lifetime, and is intimately connected with the spleen chakra. The spleen is a minor but important chakra. Your spleen plays a big part in your immune system. Just in case you're not sure where it is, it's above your waist on the left-hand side of your back. You already nurture your spleen when you put your hands on the small of your back and have a little stretch. We often do this when we need a bit of a break, when we feel tired. By doing this we're helping increase the life-energy coming into the body. So, then we feel refreshed and can carry on. This is a great little secret if you're feeling tired.

Your etheric body circulates your life-energy through your body and blood. On another level it communicates who you are. So, for example, when someone meets you and feels you're an uplifting person to be around, or when your boss sees you have great potential, they're getting this vibe from the vitality of your aura.

Believe it or not your aura contains a great deal of wisdom and knowledge about your soul's gifts, qualities, past life experiences and your soul's journey for this lifetime. Your etheric body transmits this stored information from your aura to your brain and nervous system, fashioning your physical body around it. It's almost as though you step into your body at birth, just like you'd put on a shirt or dress.

The etheric body is also known as the health aura because it's linked to your levels of vitality. It receives, transforms and transmits life-energy through every layer and level of your aura, as well as the chakras and meridians. (A meridian is a term used by traditional Chinese medicine to describe the yin and yang pathways that flow through your body—I explain these in more detail in Chapter 32.) The etheric body supplies the energy needed to sustain your physical body in peak condition. When your etheric body's *vitality* is raised, you feel healthy and vital. When it is lowered, you feel tired and depleted.

You also have a lower and higher etheric body. The lower etheric body is intricately woven into our physical body and can manifest itself in interesting ways. When a person has had a limb removed yet still feels the urge to scratch a spot where the leg or arm used to be, this is because the itch is being registered and felt in the etheric body. The communication links are still part of the person's awareness. The higher etheric body can be seen as a glowing light emanating from someone's body, creating a silhouette of light around their physical body.

If you would like to see another person's etheric body, sit opposite a friend with a blank light-coloured wall behind them. The aura near the head and top of the shoulders is the easiest to see first. So, focus on your friend's head and shoulders, gazing at the top part of their body and the wall. Soften your gaze, as if you were looking at a beautiful horizon in the distance. Don't try too hard. The moment you focus too hard on it, it will disappear! If that happens, close your eyes for a few seconds, then keep going with the exercise. The more you relax, the easier it will be.

You will notice a glowing light that may pulse in and out as the life-energy travels rapidly around your friend's body. Once you can see this luminous light around the head and shoulders, slowly move your eyes down one arm, then the other. When you notice their aura here, gradually start to move your eyes horizontally away from the body and notice what you see there. You may find the aura changes colour. Just take note of the colour. When you've finished looking horizontally left and right, start to expand your vision above your friend's head, noticing any change of colour, strength or pulsing.

Every person's aura will be different depending on the type of work they do and the relationships they are in. Even the environment you spend most time in, day or night, can affect your aura. Some people will have large auras, others small. You can also have an absent aura as well as a healthy balanced aura.

When a person has a large aura it can indicate someone who controls or dominates others, or they may be spreading themselves thin by taking on board the responsibility of others. A great example of a large magnetic spiritual aura is the Dalai Lama, an awakened person who exemplifies love, compassion and deep inner wisdom. A large aura can also reflect a healthy, balanced person who is vibrant with life-energy, happy, outgoing and optimistic with a strong sense of personal self.

A person with a smaller or absent aura may feel withdrawn, closed off from life and themselves, as though they were hiding in a shell. They will lack confidence and not want to attract attention. When the aura is absent it can indicate an unhappy person who doesn't want to be in their body—not wanting to face their pain or problems. Illness and fear can affect the shape and size of your aura.

If you're lucky you may even see the shadow of another head standing close by. Don't be alarmed. It could be an angelic guide: a close relative like an aunt or uncle, grandmother or grandfather who your friend was especially close to, who temporarily stays close forming part of their team of spirit helpers. Many guides will move in and out of an aura depending on what the person's focus is at the time. If a child dies it may choose to stay close to its mother for a period of time while they both adjust to the grief of their parting. I have even seen a mother carry the energy of her miscarried foetus in her aura.

16

Feeling drained

*I*f you're feeling lethargic, tired, off-colour, exposed, zapped, overwhelmed or weak, your etheric body needs some attention. It's a little like driving your car with a small amount of air pressure in the tyres: the car feels heavy and slow to drive, giving little to no flexibility at the wheel.

Poor health, significant trauma, substance abuse and feeling anxious for long periods of time may cause the energy of your etheric body to become separated in places from your physical body. This makes it difficult to think straight or be coordinated, as you're not feeling centred in your body. In extreme cases your eyes appear to glaze over, giving the sense that there's nobody home. Energetically speaking you're not fully present in your body.

When the etheric body is forced away from the physical body by injury or accident it will wrap itself like a sheath around the next layer in your aura—the *astral body*—dulling and masking your awareness of that layer. It's like when you have no memory after an operation or major accident. This separation of the etheric body from the physical body can also happen when people binge drink or get drunk regularly. Long-term separation from your etheric body and not being *grounded* can be a catalyst for disease. You see this when someone is leading a hectic jet-setting lifestyle or when there has been a lot of pain or abuse in a person's life that has not been addressed. A number of my clients who have experienced these situations speak of amnesia or blurred memory, confusion and difficulty with finding direction, purpose or their niche in life.

Where your thoughts go— energy will flow!

Too much energy can have the same harmful effect as too little, causing damage to your nervous system. If you're pumped up and on the go all the time it's like running all the lights and electrical appliances in your house day and night. Eventually the electrical supply burns out or shuts down. The physical body is the same; the depletion of the etheric layer affects your nervous system and adrenal glands, ultimately causing the body to close down.

Living in this high-tech age is a challenge for your etheric body. Computers, televisions, mobile phones, microwaves, plane travel, electric blankets, lights, heaters and loud sound systems all have an impact on this life-energy layer. Even household chemicals such as bleach can temporarily wipe out sections of your etheric body, especially if you are very sensitive.

There are many ways to give your etheric body a hard time. On an emotional level, if you suppress your emotions, have a tendency towards self-criticism, or get caught up in fear, worry or stress, this makes it harder for your etheric body to deliver the life-energy needed to be vital and healthy. On a mental level, if you're caught up in negative thought patterns over long periods of time that's where all the life-energy will go.

If you pay little or no attention to these issues, your etheric body can't do its job and your body is left without an energy source. And that's a bit like trying to drive a car without the steering wheel! It's impossible to have full control, function or direction.

A considerable amount of spiritual healing and clearing is done in the etheric body. When energy isn't cleared, illness develops. It's the *quality* of the etheric body that is linked to your vitality and health. This layer also has a link to your seven major energy centres, your chakras. And the chakra system—like the etheric body—receives, transforms and transmits the incoming life-energy, helping to keep you healthy and active.

Your energy

The sun is the storehouse of energy, light, heat, sound and movement for the planet and your physical and etheric bodies. You know, there's an old saying in ancient wisdom teachings: 'As above so below'. This means that just as the Earth and the universe receives the sun's energy, so do we.

The sun gives out three different types of energy. The first is *fire*, or an electrical type of energy, which is converted into heat, light, sound, magnetism, colour, vibration and motion. The second type is *prana*. If you look carefully you can see the vitality of prana in the air we breathe. Next time you're at the beach on a sunny day, gaze at the point where the horizon meets the water. Relax and let your eyes go slightly out of focus, as if you were going to view a 3D picture. You'll notice tiny silvery sperm-like wrigglers (vitality globules) moving across the sky. When you see this you are actually seeing life-energy in the air we breathe, which has been vitalised by the sun. It's really exciting when you see these little globules for the first time.

The third type of energy coming from the sun's rays is *kundalini* (serpent fire), the fire of your own life-energy. It sits curled up like a snake at the bottom of your spine. When the kundalini is released it travels up the spine like two intertwining snakes. This image, also known as the caduceus, appears on signs at some older pharmacies and medical suppliers. When you take a closer look at the intertwined snakes you'll see how they look like the double helix of DNA structure. As the energies cross and rise, they meet at junction points—the chakras—indicating a fusion of two opposing and opposite forces: the masculine and feminine.

Prana simply means life-energy—it is the breath of life.

You are more miraculous and intricate than you could imagine. Your network of subtle energies delicately weaves its way in and out, up and through your physical body. It supplies all the energy to your cells, muscles and organs.

Now we've had a look at your etheric body and the wonderful work it does, and the supply of your energy source, why not have a go at sensing and supporting your life-energy with the following quick re-energising exercise?

Re-energise your body

Do this exercise outside in the sun for ten minutes with your shoes off and your feet touching the Earth or under a tree with your feet on some grass.

- Sitting or lying down, connect your feet or body to the Earth.
- Begin to visualise a small whirling centre of energy about 4 centimetres in width over your spleen organ (just above the waist on the left-hand side, at the back). This is where your spleen chakra is located.
- Breathe into this spleen chakra, taking the breath deep into your lower abdomen.
- Now visualise the second chakra near the diaphragm (this is just above the spleen on the right-hand side of your back). Connect the spleen with the diaphragm using a golden thread of light.
- Then visualise the third and last part of your golden triangle: the centre above your heart over the thymus gland.
- As you continue to breathe in and relax, see a golden link now being made between all three chakras, emulating the natural flow of the pranic triangle.
- Continue to breathe into this flowing triangle of energy, filling its centre now with light and love.
- Visualise the energy travelling around the chakras three times, just like the wisdom of your body's intelligence does naturally.
- You may or may not feel the energy moving around, but if you do it every day for a week I'll bet you will notice a difference. If you don't happen to be sensitive to energy as yet, know that with intention it is automatically done. That's the beauty of this work: *energy follows thought*. It is a powerful exercise.

Continue to stay in this relaxed state for 5–10 minutes to let the energy balance and settle in your body.

Energy follows thought

This is a wonderful way to stimulate your immune system, charging up the old batteries! It can be especially helpful if you are suffering from immune deficiencies of any kind, or are generally just low in energy. Strengthening the etheric body creates cohesion and alignment of all your subtle layers, while at the same time it re-energises the physical body, so you feel healthy, vital and alive.

17

How you act you attract

Life is extraordinary. I remember a beautiful telephone conversation I had with my dear uncle many years ago. He wanted to know what I was doing in my life now I had moved interstate. He became very curious when I spoke about the varied experiences I'd had as an energetic and spiritual healer. I was half expecting him to disapprove, but instead he started to chuckle, saying he'd like to tell *me* a story about him and my dad. It turned out that during all the chattering, tinkering and beers my dad and uncle shared in the back shed, they were questioning the meaning of life and what happens after death.

Uncle Brian told me of a secret pact the two of them made. The first person to die was to resolve the mystery of life beyond the grave by paying the other a visit! Tears began to roll down my cheeks—I couldn't believe what I was hearing. It turned out that several days after my dad died, my uncle awoke from his sleep to see my dad sitting on the end of his bed, just as he used to look in the days of their fortnightly visits. My uncle was a little shocked to say the least. But just as my uncle was getting over his shock and about to ask some questions, he heard Dad say, 'Oh, Brian not you too!' It turned out that the fear and shock my uncle had registered on seeing Dad was a contributing factor to Dad's energy fading away. My uncle said he always regretted that the moment was so fleeting. He felt disappointed at not being able to be there for my dad.

As it turned out, my uncle worked with a spiritualist who explained how Dad appeared to him and why he faded away. From that moment my uncle never feared death. Death wasn't an end to who we are in life, but a transformation into another state of being. I couldn't believe my uncle hadn't shared his experience until thirty-two years later. It touched my heart, validating all the times I had seen Dad in my waking dreams, in healing sessions, meditations and the sense of him beside me when driving home from college some nights. It's sad that we don't often share these important stories. So, my uncle could see Dad, because he was still able to move from place to place after his physical death in what is known as our *astral body*, also referred to as the emotional/desire body.

The astral body, the second energy layer that surrounds us, is sometimes referred to as a vehicle, suggesting travel. This is appropriate because our astral body *can* travel. Many people do a lot of night travelling while they sleep. The interesting thing is that sometimes the memory is so strong you can clearly recall the people and places you saw in your dream state. When you come across that exact same place or person in your waking state it's like you are having a déjà vu moment. Very curious. If you remember flying in a dream that's when you were astral travelling.

I was visiting my son a few years ago and had exactly one of those déjà vu moments. Being unfamiliar with the city and the route that my son took after he picked me up from the airport, I sat back and enjoyed the ride, travelling through the outskirts of the city centre in peak hour. I took in the up and down winding roadways, the one-way streets and the beautiful jacaranda trees in full bloom, but that's it.

During the night, in my sleep state, I flew over land and water, taking in an aerial view of some large three-storey houses built by a marina. I remembered being so excited that I had the hang of this flying business. Feeling confident, I decided to more closely investigate the pleasure cruisers moored in the marina. I ducked and weaved in between the boats, looking through the portholes, noting the smaller craft and the gentle movement of the inky blue water. I was having a great time. I could even recall the thoughts I had in that dream state the next morning. It was so vivid. At one point I picked up a lady passenger at a bus-stop and placed her on my back, indicating that she needed to hold on tight around my throat or else she'd fall. My mission was to take her home, as it wasn't her time to leave her husband just yet. I explained that it was important that she return home now, as he was waiting for her. All the next day I felt perky and happy, if not a little bemused, and buzzed with energy.

It was on my return journey to the airport a week later that I had my déja vu experience. My son decided to take a different route, showing me the outer city suburbs he thought I might like. Fifteen minutes into the journey there it was—the place in my dream: the houses, the marina, the winding road and the bus-stop. The exact boats that I had been so curious about in my dream state were there in front of me, moored at the marina. I couldn't believe it. Overjoyed, I smiled to myself. It was a great validation of my night flight. It was as though I knew that area intimately without having ever been there physically.

The astral body is able to move away from the sleeping physical body with great agility and speed over long distances, even though it remains connected to your physical body by an astral cord. It is not dissimilar to the umbilical cord that connects a newborn baby to its mother. This cord enables your astral energy to come back to your physical body in the waking state. Have you ever felt your physical body shudder or jump just before you fully wake up? This can be your astral body coming back suddenly into your physical body from an uncomfortable dream.

Our astral body is an exact carbon copy of our physical body, but it has a denseness about it that enables it to be seen by untrained eyes. When you see an image of a person who has just died, you are seeing their astral body. Many people have witnessed this but often have no understanding, so they disregard it. This is what was happening to my uncle when he saw my dad. If you have a clear understanding of the astral body, its potential and limitations, this will assist you when you die, helping you understand the many states of being that you may find. Further reading on the astral states after death can be found in the *Tibetan Book of Living and Dying*.

The astral body is like a storehouse of our positive and negative moods, passions, desires, feelings, fears, anger, resentment and jealousies—a reservoir of emotions. Because water has the capacity to store memory and because our body is made up of 70 per cent water, our astral body is the container of all our past and present emotional experiences. This is also why cells hold memory. These stored memories are like the *energetic footprints of our emotional scars, trauma and abuse.* This reservoir of stored information extends way beyond this life, connecting us back to our ancient ancestors. We carry their memories, their triumphs and tragedies in our cells, in our astral body. These deep-seated memories can disturb or enhance our health.

When you reflect back on the personality or psychological traits of the previous three generations of your family, you will start to find some interesting patterns that have been carried forward. There may be issues around self-esteem, abandonment, abuse of power or of courage and inspiration. You may find you relate to a young child in the family or to the traits of an old cousin, aunt or uncle. You may act, say or do things or copy their mannerisms without being aware of it. This connection comes from stored memory in your energy body and cells.

So how does this all work? Your astral body lies 6–20 centimetres out from your physical body, depending on a person's awareness, personal development, and past life experiences. It acts like a bridge between the subtle layers of your aura and your physical body. The feelings you have are experienced first in your astral body, then your physical body. These feelings are then absorbed into your cells. The memories in your cells impact on your brain, your thoughts, and how good you feel about yourself. This is why *your emotions can and do influence your physical body and your health.*

The planets affect you as well. For example, if you were to take a brief look at how the moon affects the tides of huge bodies of water, you would become more aware of how the moon influences your own 'sea of emotions'. It's something you can check out for yourself when *your* boat gets a little rocky. Try to observe what triggers your sea of emotions in the physical environment for future reference. We all feel inside us the highs and lows of our emotional self, finding it difficult sometimes to contain the brewing storms that overwhelm us. The feeling is a bit like being in a small boat cast out to sea in high tides. We never know what is going to get washed up. Note the interesting information brought forth over the last century regarding the lunar phases and women's menstrual cycles—another connection to water and fluid.

If the moon can affect your emotions and the way you behave and view the world, it can certainly influence and affect another sea of fluid: the blood and its hormones. The cyclical nature of the lunar phases can parallel the natural cycles of a woman's ovulation and fertility. The life of a woman intimately mirrors Mother Earth's cycles of the seasons: birth, growth, maturation and death.

The astral body is highly magnetic, naturally drawing to it whatever feelings and emotions you are experiencing. As we know, fear attracts fear, love attracts love. When your negative emotions are running high it can feel like you are swimming in a thick pea soup or are on a merry-go-round cranked up to full speed. Because the magnetised energy is stronger around you at these times, it can leave you feeling tired, weak and spun out to dry—literally! So, it's really important you're aware of the emotions you're getting caught up in. They can make life a hundred times better or worse, depending on where you're at. A positive emotion can leave you feeling joyous and happy for hours.

If you've been wondering and questioning why things keep happening a certain way in your life, take a moment to reflect on your recent thoughts, desires, wishes, even fears. Become aware of just how instrumental and clever you've been in manifesting or attracting those things good, bad and indifferent to you. You'll be surprised at what you discover.

Thoughts are energy

Spend a little time identifying your fears, then start to work actively towards dispelling them. It will help you turn unhelpful situations around. This is an important step because dominant emotions, such as love or fear, have a huge impact—not just on you, but on the planet. At the moment, many decisions people and nations are making are being made out of fear. The power of this fear comes from your astral body. Imagine how different life would be if you were focusing on love and hope. Thoughts are energy. Astral energy has a strong impact on the physical body. Depending on how powerful the thoughts are, their positive or negative effects upon the astral plane can take on a life of their own, leaving you feeling dominated or drained by them.

However, not all things astral are negative. Due to its magnetism, the astral holds much promise when used for such healing qualities as love, peace and harmony. It is a state of being where we can connect and sort out our relationships with those that have departed this Earth plane. We can even visit our much-loved pets.

Not long after I had cancer I returned to a place where I used to live. There I caught up with an old friend who had taken my position at the aged-care facility where I'd once worked. She offered me a healing treatment and I jumped at the chance. Once on the table, I was surprised at how quickly I fell into a deep relaxed state. What felt like fifteen minutes was in fact one and a half hours. During that healing session my energy was raised to a level on the astral plane where I was able to see my parents, who were both deceased. We communicated telepathically to each other about our unresolved issues. They spoke about their love and wishes for my future, apologised for the difficult times, and told me that the decision I had made to move to a new city with my family was the right one. Being in this deep state of peace, knowing that I had been loved and was still being loved across the ether by my parents, allowed me to let go and forgive. The suppressed tears of sadness and grief I had held onto for years now flowed effortlessly. I left that day feeling supported beyond the grave, letting go of a burden I had carried for years. It was a heightened positive and empowering experience, proving to me that life does go on, and tremendous healing on the astral plane can still be done between people even after death. I had magnetised to me with loving intent the exact healing situation and energy needed at that time for my and my parents' healing.

So as we think and act— we attract!

18

The storehouse of your thoughts

*E*lise had an active, inquisitive mind and found it difficult to still her persistent thoughts. She had a great sense of what was right or wrong in the world and found herself in a compromised situation where she felt violated by a professional practitioner during a treatment. It led to Elise feeling sexually violated. She left the premises vulnerable, angry and frustrated at the perpetrator. Making it worse, the appropriate channels of authority didn't really have the time or energy to listen to her story.

Months had passed and her constant thoughts of anger, revenge, hate and injustice became toxic, threatening to ruin her life. Elise understood what was happening to her, and even though she had been through the appropriate channels, the patience required for justice to prevail seemed little compensation to stop the overload of mental thoughts she was still experiencing.

Assessing Elise's aura, her continual angry thoughts and strong negative emotions looked like a watery potato sack encasing her torso. It was as though her mental and astral bodies had merged in a sea of toxic substance. Fortunately for Elise she was able to see just how powerful her mental thoughts were and how they affected her physical body. She had constant bronchitis and felt like she was drowning in her own fluidic emotions. Her body was giving her clear signs that she needed to let go. And as all avenues for justice had been explored, it was well and truly time to address the aftermath of her thoughts that were making her sick.

Sometimes it's easy to forget how powerful thoughts are; how they impact on and are influenced by your third energy field—the *mental body*. This is where your higher self/soul finds its expression.

The mental body has two entirely different roles to play. The first is connected to your personality and lower mind, known as the conscious mind. Its second role is that of the higher mind, which connects us to the energy of our soul, and all its wonderful creativity.

The mental body is where you store your thoughts and beliefs. Even your awareness impacts on these thoughts and beliefs. Your mental body is concerned with all the knowledge you have accumulated, and how you create, process and organise your thoughts. How you think about a dog or cat, country or religion is dealt with through your mental body.

This body is 7.5–20 centimetres from your physical body and it can be seen in the aura as yellow. Your mental body is connected to your solar plexus chakra, known as your concrete or conscious mind. This is the logical, rational and analytical thinking mind you use in everyday life. Your mental body is wired in such a way that when you think thoughts they are stepped down, just like you might step down a staircase. So, as thoughts descend from our mental body they wrap themselves in astral/emotional material. Put simply, these thoughts are influenced and coloured by your emotions. Once wrapped in emotions your thoughts further step down into your etheric body. Here they connect with your library of stored memory patterns. So, your thoughts are then influenced by past experiences, good and bad. Then, finally, your thoughts enter your brain. During this stepping down process your thoughts gather positive or negative energy as they pass through the different layers of your aura. That's why thoughts are so powerful and can pack such a punch.

As Buddha tells us: 'You are what you think'. The great gift is that once you understand how influential your thoughts are in your life, you can use this information to your advantage. A good first step is to become less attached to your thoughts about yourself, because the way you think about yourself can become entrenched or wired. Then, basically you imprison yourself in a certain image that you feel you have to live up to. The great news is that you can change your thought patterns right now. What recurring thoughts are tripping you up? Do you need to stop putting yourself down? Or perhaps you don't see yourself as loveable or clever enough, not young enough, not rich enough, or maybe you're always thinking things won't turn out well. Whatever your thoughts are be careful they're not holding you back. As you can literally rewire yourself, you can create different outcomes. I wonder what negative thought you might like to change right now to a positive one about yourself.

Humans are still developing their mental bodies. We are learning about the power and responsibility of our thoughts, along with the impact that our attitudes and beliefs have on every living thing, whether that be a person, place or object.

To get a sense of what is possible, you might like to look at Dr Masaru Emoto's work with water, which he has studied at a crystalline level. When polluted water is prayed over, for example, the distorted crystals in the water start to heal. When Dr Emoto took a water sample and placed it in different test tubes, those samples which had uplifting words taped to their test tube became more beautiful, and vice versa. This was a significant finding as we too are made of water.

Part of getting on top of your mental body is in learning to control the thoughts that you emanate. Just as you can suffer from the emotions that flow from your astral body, ones that keep overwhelming you, you can experience the same thing with your mental body.

Have you ever had persistent thoughts where you felt you were going crazy if your mind didn't stop? It can be paralysing when your thoughts go into overdrive. So, it is important to practise stilling the mind, and being conscious of the way you think. Learning to meditate or relax, or getting out for a walk, can help you chill out.

It's important to see when you're being negative and how destructive this is in relationships with your family, friends and colleagues. To become aware of your mental body, start to pay attention to the thousands of thoughts you have in one day. You'll be surprised. Then you can begin to see how many of those thoughts were positive and how many were negative.

There's an easy exercise you can do to monitor your thoughts and break bad habits. Place a *loose* thick rubber band around your wrist. Every time you have a negative thought during the day give it a ping. It hurts, but it's a great way to become aware of when you're being destructive. Arthur Powell, author and educator of the Ageless Wisdom Teachings, tells us that 'concentration will fashion the mind into an instrument that can be used at will to the owner' but it is the exercise of meditation that will support and refocus your mind chatter.

When you look at the mental body, it's interesting to see how it can dominate your aura. People who live in their heads have a lot of yellow in their aura, as opposed to those who get very emotional, who have more orange in their aura. If a person is giving a mentally stimulating talk, for instance, the yellow in their aura will increase. In many cases it may have a golden luminous hue if someone is talking about spiritual matters. I have even seen a distinct yellow circle form around someone's throat chakra, in response to their passionate presentation at a seminar. This reminded me just how much our auras change constantly depending on what we are doing, speaking, thinking or creating at any point in time.

There are lots of ways to experience the power of thought in a mind/body way. I use the following simple example with students to show the power that a single word can have on a person. I ask them to shut their eyes and experience the feelings and sensations they get in their body as I say the word *fear*, pause, then say the word *love*. Try these same words yourself or get a friend to say them aloud for you. *Fear*—pause and wait a moment while you sense and feel the energetic impact of the word. Then proceed to *love*. When the students open their eyes they are amazed at the profound effect these words have on their body. When they hear the word fear their energy contracted, they felt heavy and restricted. When they heard the word love, they felt expanded, open and light.

This simple exercise demonstrates the power of the spoken word. It makes the whole concept of energy more tangible and relatable. It's not just the spoken word you need to be aware of. When a negative thought is held long term in the mental body, it is also the impact it has in your aura. Negativity can eventually cause illness. However, when you change or shift your negative thoughts or attitudes a healing process begins.

So, how do you think?

When I am reading a client's energy, the position of their mental thought-form and its colour, texture, size and shape all give me valuable information about negative beliefs or attitudes trapped in their aura.

Thoughts are things—be mindful of what you choose.

One of the ways thoughts become stagnant in your mental body is when you have fixed attitudes of how things should be in your life, particularly at a certain time in your life.

When this is the case, you set yourself up with no room to grow. By putting on mental blinkers, your capacity to think and have vision narrows. Mental pain and suffering follow because you are blocking or trying to contain the natural flow of energy. Energy is meant to flow. When you block this energy, you also hinder your personal development. Can you imagine how clogged your mental body would become if you couldn't turn your thoughts off?

When I see persistent negative thought-forms that look like a dark, stormy cloud around a client's head, the client often describes their problem as being stuck in their head. They speak of confusion, difficulties with concentration, and lack of clarity.

We are all mentally wired differently. Have you ever wondered why a friend can pick up a new concept and run with it, while you're left wondering what it's all about? Your thoughts and the way you process information is unique. Some people are more *mental* types, so they have a quicker and faster capacity for processing information. Others need time to sit with their thoughts. Our mental bodies operate differently.

<h1 style="text-align:center">19</h1>

Gateway to the divine

Many years after my first few encounters with angels I attended a workshop specifically on angels. Having had my own experiences with angels during some difficult times, I had been left with many questions still unanswered. Because I was inspired by the loving and nurturing I had felt with those visitations, it encouraged me to discover more about their ability to uplift your spirits. I had been fascinated with the lightness and luminosity I saw and felt in my energy at that time.

I was attracted to the workshop because the facilitator seemed to be an ambassador for angels on Earth. After the workshop there was a long queue of people waiting to get their angel books signed. It was quite frenetic and not at all angelic, everyone was rushing and pushing to get in line. And I was one of them! Funnily enough, the closer I got to the table where the signing was to take place the calmer I became. My busy thoughts were fading. The noise and din made by the hundreds of people leaving the auditorium felt like it was being slowed down and hushed, like a baby being lulled to sleep. When it was my turn, I was drawn to the eyes of the facilitator. They danced and sparkled like moonbeams on a deep blue crystal lake. Her energy felt open and wide, fully expanded like wings of light. In that instant, as our eyes met, I felt spiritually massaged with divine love. I felt the illumined energy of her extended aura, open like arms outstretched to greet me. They were filled with loving light. I cherished the moment as I floated home.

At the outer edge of your aura are your spiritual energy bodies. These outer layers are like delicate, clear fine crystal and can be sensed or felt up to 50 centimetres beyond the physical body. When a person's spiritual bodies are active, you sense this when you meet them. You have a feeling of being uplifted, a feeling of love, openness or kindness. After even a chance encounter with someone with this type of energy, you may feel inspired or encouraged to move through a difficult time, simply because the person's aura has affected your aura in a positive way. Their energy is so elevated it lifts yours as well. Or perhaps you've heard yourself saying when so and so came into the room it seemed to light up. Some may even call these friends or acquaintances Earth angels.

Our *spiritual bodies* vibrate at a very high frequency. They are gossamer fine, yet very strong. Depending on the person, these bodies can feel light and clear. To get an idea of how thick or dense these energy bodies are, we could compare them to a clear drinking glass. The thicker the glass the heavier and denser it looks and feels. This is the same for the energy bodies or part of the aura that is closer to the physical body. The further out from the physical body the layers of the aura are the finer they become. Working with these finer bodies can feel like moving in the presence of celestial angels. They are part of your aura, but the quality and type of their composition is totally different. When I work on people as an energetic healer it's not unusual for me to come into contact with the client's angelic guide, giving proof that no matter how tricky life gets we never travel alone.

The etheric, astral and mental bodies we have already looked at exist for only one lifetime or incarnation, just like your physical body, whereas your spiritual bodies exist for many lifetimes. They are the immortal parts. That's why *energy cannot die. It is simply transformed* into a higher vibration or state of being. This happens because light influences the structure of your body's atoms and molecules. The more you connect with the immense light held in your spiritual body, the more this light will influence your life in a positive way. It's like changing to a higher wattage light bulb.

When I speak about spiritual bodies I am not talking about your personality but of the beauty, love and light of your spirit or divine essence. These spiritual bodies contain your divine purpose. They also contain information about your soul's qualities and gifts, and your past lives. After death you exist in your astral body. Once you have worked through your desires, you exist in your spiritual or heavenly body. Between lives this body sustains you in whatever heaven means for you, relevant to your beliefs, culture and religious views. *Whether you choose to believe in an afterlife or not, your level of consciousness will still exist.*

Contained within your spiritual body are three different energy levels. The first connects you to your intuition. Often *intuitive thoughts* seem to appear out of nowhere, when in fact they come from your all-wise spiritual body. We've all had those sudden inspirational moments. When this first started to happen to me, I was a little confused. Intuition is an important part of energy healing because it enables you to pick up on what is happening for a client. I find that what I say to people doesn't come from me per se, but through me, like a door opening and shutting. Once I have said what I needed to say to the person, I instantly forget the phrase or sentence. I feel quite stupid, especially when they ask me to repeat the sentence a few minutes later, because it's gone. When you learn to trust your own intuition remarkable things will begin to happen. You feel joy, confidence and excitement, as though you have just connected with a long-lost friend. Your options and choices can feel endless. You may feel a great sense of hope and trust in the future where once there was despair.

The second level of your spiritual body is that of your *spiritual will*, which is connected to your life purpose. As you have free will it's up to you to activate your spiritual will. You do this by listening to your heart's desire, the voice of your soul. If you want to activate your spiritual will, take a few minutes to be with yourself everyday while you contemplate 'Who am I?' and 'What's the purpose of my life?'. Learn to be relaxed and patient and the answers will come with practice.

Intuition comes from a higher source that is in all of us.

The third level of your spiritual body is your *universal* or *cosmic level*. This connects you to the oneness of God within, your divinity. One of the ways to connect to the oneness of God is to be in nature. Many of us feel our spirits are uplifted when we walk in a natural bushland setting or a beautiful garden. My friend and I had just completed a four-day Kalachara Retreat with the Dalai Lama and when the program came to a close, we had this incredible desire to leave the venue and visit the adjacent park. In our uplifted state from all the chanting and heartfelt words of the Dalai Lama, we commented to each other that we could each feel our hearts beating loudly in our chests. We were amazed at the intensity of the energy, considering our seats were in the back row of the large venue.

As we walked in the warmth of the mid-afternoon sun we came across a massive Moreton Bay fig tree. It was there we decided to lie on the ground, using the fallen leaves as a blanket. Moreton Bay fig trees have exposed root systems that appear to course endlessly under their large canopies. It didn't take long for my friend and me to nestle comfortably between the trees roots and become still.

As we closed our eyes and bathed in the filtered sunlight that gently warmed our bodies, we began to feel the energy of the Earth below us. It was mirroring our heartbeats. Its vibration, however, was slower and deeper. As we began to slow our breathing, and breathe in sync with the Earth below, it felt like our auras and hearts were expanding and melding with that of the tree, Earth, sunlight and the chirping birds tucked among the branches' foliage. In that moment we both felt the oneness and connection to all that is. Those few brief minutes seemed a lifetime.

To feel the oneness of life our spiritual bodies experience all the time, we need to open our hearts and connect with the beauty that surrounds us. We can all do this by being in nature, or by doing creative activities that lift and inspire the soul. All the arts—including music, painting, dancing and writing—help to purify the aura from our attachments and desires. Shortly you will see how these spiritual bodies fit into the bigger picture of your aura.

20

Chakra power

Now you've got a sense of what your aura is about, let's take a look at your chakras. There are seven major chakras (energy centres) in your body. Like the layers of your aura, your chakras have a powerful effect on your life. Your chakras are located in the first energy layer—the etheric layer—of your aura. They stretch from the bottom of your spine to the top of your head. The word chakra comes from Sanskrit and means 'wheel'. This refers to the fact that each chakra is a whirling vortex of energy that carries within its life-energy the blueprint of your soul's journey.

Your chakras are like small memory chips. They contain the memory of your lives past and present. These memories are made up from your thoughts and experiences through time. Every moment of your day you are registering, creating and storing information in this delicate system. Your chakras act like filters through which you view the world. So, if your emotions have been crushed growing up, or in subsequent relationships,

Figure 2: Your seven major chakras

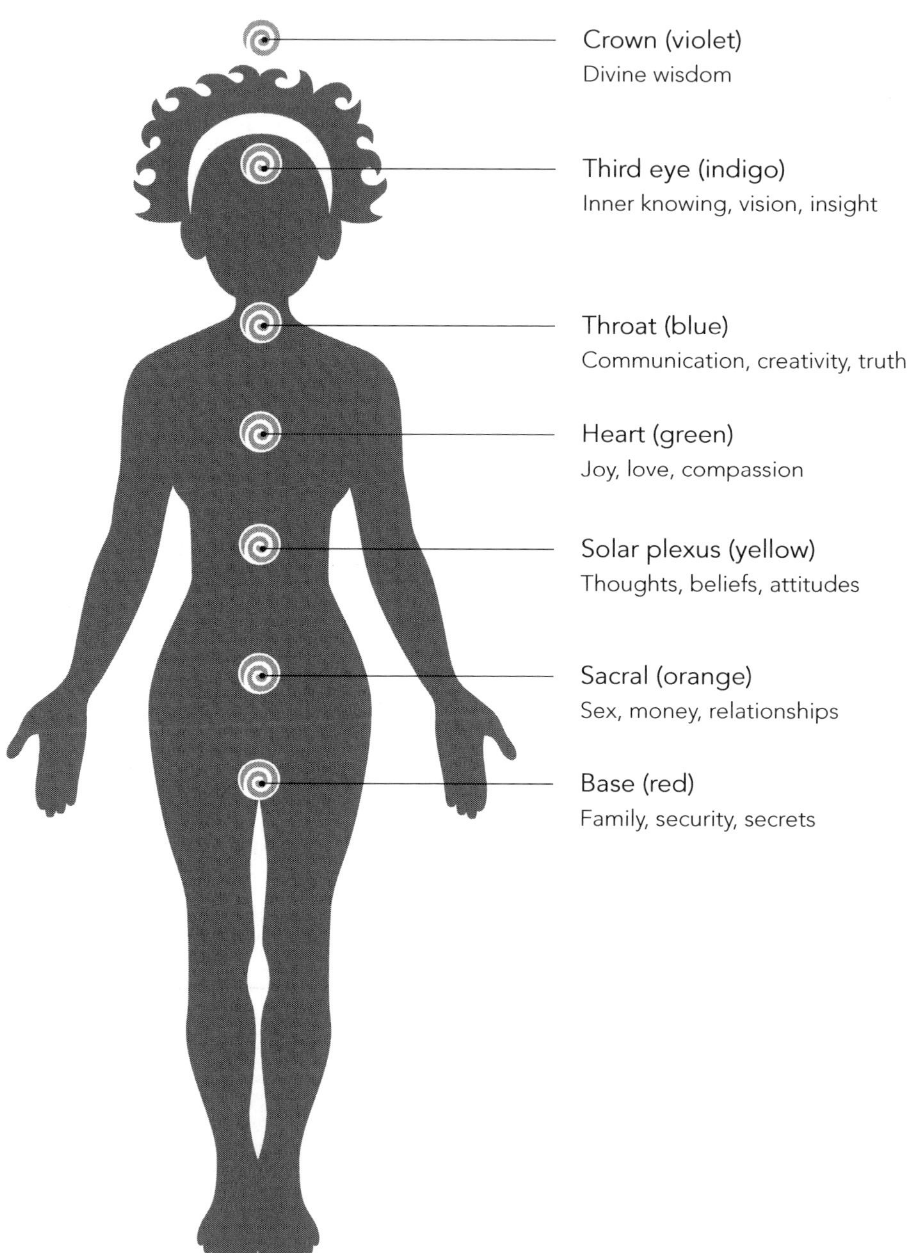

most likely you'll respond to others very differently than those who don't have these emotional issues.

Our chakras are also like magnets. They draw life-energy into your body. As energy is always moving, your chakras also radiate energy outwards from your body into your aura, and out into the world. As a result, your chakras constantly interact with the environment you live, breathe, work and play in. Part of their job is also to filter, transmit and receive information about the world around you. They are like psychic generators that distribute incoming and outgoing information into your aura. In an ideal situation the life energies that come together bring balance and harmony.

Chakras can vary in size from that of a fifty cent piece upwards. They are like the layers of an onion. How well your chakras operate depends on your beliefs and awareness, and whether or not you're in harmony and balance with yourself. Unless you peel back the immediate layers of your chakras, you will never know the richness inside, and so you'll never discover your full potential. When you do peel back the layers of your life it can be a little challenging to look at your baggage, but well worth the effort when you can recognise your issues and move on. Think of the enhanced flavour, aroma and body an onion can give to your culinary delights. Understanding your chakras is exactly the same: they can both make you cry, but it's worth it in the end!

You experience the everyday world through your lower three chakras. While your upper three chakras connect you to your spiritual self, your heart chakra lies in the middle and links these two parts. It is your bridge between your daily life and the life of your soul. Without putting your heart into what you do, life can be pretty flat and mundane. However, when you do put your heart into everything you undertake, you infuse your days with new life, real passion and spirit.

The chakras

First chakra (base of spine)—your foundations = family, security, secrets = how you trust.

Second chakra (sacral, reproductive area)—your emotions, desire, sexual expression, money, relationships, creative self, authority and control = how you relate to the world around you.

Third chakra (solar plexus, stomach)—personal power, intellect, self-confidence, self-esteem, self-worth = how you define yourself through your thoughts, beliefs and attitudes.

Fourth Chakra (heart)—self-love, compassion, peace, unconditional love = how you love.

Fifth chakra (throat)—self-expression, personal creativity = how you communicate and speak your truth.

Sixth chakra (third eye)—intuition, vision, ability to see the big picture = how you see life.

Seventh chakra (crown)—wisdom, connection to the divine, bliss = how you connect to your divinity.

Once you learn to sense each chakra, it can feel hot or cold, tingly or like pins and needles to the touch. Like your aura, your chakras have much to reveal. When I'm working on clients who are run down, I often feel a drawing sensation in my hand, because the energy in their chakras is very low—it's as if the life-energy has been sucked out of them. Chakras can be torn, jagged, ripped, explosive, leaky, expanded, heavy, toxic or distorted. This happens when you are tired or overstretched, when you're not living the life that feeds you, when you're in an unsupportive relationship, and so on.

Chakras can be open or closed at any time. When they are open, the life-energy flows freely through them. That's when you might experience a sense of openness, and feel more outgoing and positive in your work, relationships and family life. When your chakras are closed, your personal energy becomes stagnant, and can end up making you feel sick, over-concerned about issues in life, worried or fretful. That's when you feel stuck, confused, and unable to interact with others.

Each chakra vibrates and spins in different directions. A chakra may spin slowly or extremely fast, depending on its location in the body. The higher up on your body or the more spiritual a chakra is, the faster it spins, because spiritual energy moves faster and is lighter than the energy you experience in your everyday life. When your chakras are seriously out of balance you are ruled by your addictions, desires and unhelpful behaviours. It's not a good idea to work directly on just one chakra, as you could overstimulate that energy centre and cause imbalance and harm. As they're all linked, your chakras need to be worked on as a whole.

21
Chakras in practice

When a client describes an area of discomfort in their body, an energetic healer will look at the person's aura and what it may tell them energetically. The client's past history is *always* relevant to their present situation. So, when a client says, 'I have always suffered with stomach upsets, poor digestion and have recently been diagnosed with irritable bowel syndrome', the energy healer will relate this to the solar plexus chakra, which corresponds to issues about self-confidence, self-worth or self-criticism.

A sore back around the heart area, and twinges in a person's right or left arm and shoulder blade, can direct us to heart-chakra issues about your ability to be kind, loving, compassionate and forgiving towards yourself. It can also extend to matters of the heart around anger and betrayal stored from past relationships. This area is also connected to the thymus gland and our immune system. If the solar plexus is blocked, the energy to the heart will also be blocked, impeding the flow of energy in both directions up and down the chakra system.

If there is tightness in and around the hip area, this can relate to the sacral chakra, and issues about personal power in relationships, sex, money, control and our ability to be creative.

Poor circulation in the legs or feet, and aching calf muscles can relate to the base chakra and issues that involve family, trust, fear, survival, identity and will. So, our bodies reveal a great deal about what is going on for us.

When Jenny came to see me she described herself as sceptical about energy healing. However, her need to have another baby outweighed her scepticism. Though only in her late thirties, Jenny had been told she was peri-menopausal and the likelihood of her having a baby was nil. This was creating tremendous grief for her. At the onset of our first session she told me she wasn't too interested in what a chakra, aura or the like was, she was a Christian girl who had her beliefs. Not a problem, I assured her. After listening to her baby story, Jenny eagerly hopped on the table.

The blocked energetic patterns of the client will relate to areas of their physical body where they are experiencing pain, discomfort or illness.

I used a physical therapy called Bowen Technique on Jenny. Starting with the basic gentle movements on her lower back, I could feel where Jenny was holding her grief and sadness. It was at the base of her spine, in the base chakra, which is related to family, fear and trust. As I slowly moved up and down her body I became increasingly aware of each of the chakras and meridians that were storing blocked energy. Her body was stiff and rigid. There was little dialogue at that first session, and Jenny coped really well. She enjoyed a sense of peace and relaxation she hadn't felt for a long time. I suggested she take home some Bach Flower Remedies to take through the coming weeks, to support the emotional shifts during this transitional period.

At the next visit Jenny was ready to discuss the grief and loss that I had picked up on previously. We continued with Bowen. Jenny felt safe now to open up about the loss of her father and brother and the circumstances surrounding their deaths. She was devastated by their close passing and spoke about the emptiness and void she felt. Trying to hold the family together through this time of trauma was becoming burdensome. As I continued to work on Jenny's body, she continued to honour her feelings. The stored frozen memories locked in her cells began to release. Jenny had closed her feelings down. There didn't appear to be much time for her after helping her mum and the family her brother had left behind. She felt guilty if she took time out. The areas of Jenny's body where she had denied her feelings were where the flow of life-energy had stopped. Her chakras were depleted and she was nursing a broken heart.

Over a three-month period, Jenny looked forward to our time together unravelling and gently addressing the energetic issues connected to her body and chakras. The grief about not having a baby that she spoke of in her first session was in fact masking a bigger issue: the loss of her father and brother and the grief she felt as a result.

The last session I saw Jenny was memorable. She was glowing; her life-energy had returned in abundance and she was overwhelmingly positive and bright. Jenny was pregnant! She brought her healthy, beautiful baby girl for a visit ten months later.

22

Sorting family and security issues

Mark looked like a bomb had gone off in and around his genitals. His base chakra appeared to have had a paint pot spilt on it, leaving a dark, heavy and toxic splattered pattern with sharp jagged edges. When Mark began to talk he described his immense difficulty with wanting to live. It was hard for him to pay attention to his needs and he was not happy in his current job. He was not sure who he was anymore, but was keen to find out. As he told me his life story, a pattern of needing constant change and being dissatisfied at work and in relationships, and with people in general, became evident. His voice was sullen and sad, his eyes were all over the place and he was fidgety and avoided eye contact. He was not feeling comfortable in his body on many different levels. He was here, there and everywhere in his life. I was very aware of his scattered life-energy.

Mark then spoke about 'not wanting to be here'. He felt confused and guilty about these thoughts because there were people who had considerably less. He felt worthless and he wasn't sure what he was in the world for. He didn't feel he belonged, and had a strong sense of not fitting into his family. This pattern of not fitting in had also extended to his work, and his peer and social groups. In a funny way he felt fraudulent. Mark was also aware of not wanting to be in his physical body, and though his hectic life seemed like a whole lot of fun initially, he was now scared and fearful about the future. He had thoughts of suicide but couldn't bring himself to do it. Unable to stabilise his mood swings, Mark felt he was hanging by a thread between life and death. He didn't feel anchored or grounded in life. He had strong past life recall. Mark was a very sensitive soul.

Interestingly, Mark's story mirrored many of those of the clients I've seen who were well-educated, intelligent, hardworking professional people, often high achievers, and in many cases perfectionists. The overriding theme, however, was that of feeling disgruntled and rejected, cold and distant, and disillusioned about the work they did and themselves. This lack of connection they had with themselves reflected the way they saw the world. It was the same for Mark. He simply couldn't connect to himself, as it felt overwhelmingly painful to try to do so. He had reached a point of dissatisfaction with who he was and his environment, everything seemed painful.

To the energetic practitioner, base-chakra issues and a feeling of lack of control in the client's life suggest old wounds created at a time when the person had *no* control over their life. It can be a classic sign of abuse on any level.

In Mark's case, his issues went back to his early childhood experiences. Secrets about family sexual abuse, not being heard as a child, being abandoned or rejected, poor bonding or abuse from one or more parents, are all part of base-chakra wounding. We all need love as a base or foundation to thrive, and lack of love is a major issue for those with problems around their base chakra. Young adults with strong base-chakra dysfunction find it very hard, if not impossible, to sustain healthy relationships. And because of what they've had to deal with, there is generally a huge suppression of anger, which looks like an *implosion*.

When I clairvoyantly see cords attached to the base chakra this often means there has been abuse. The information I obtain from the cords is held in the body's cellular memory. Sadly, abuse is a common theme in young clients aged twenty-seven to thirty-eight years old. What they have suppressed throughout their early adolescence seems to resurface between these ages. While it's unsettling for them to revisit their pain, it's an opportunity to begin the healing process. Recreational drugs are often used to deal with this pain, which only adds to the confusion and chaos clients find themselves in.

Our unaddressed emotions, thoughts and feelings we don't take responsibility for are reflected back to us through the people and situations we encounter in our daily lives.

Another intriguing aspect of base-chakra problems is that people often carry wounds common to their race, colour or creed, where there has been a strong dominance of one sex over the other. When people migrate to another country, or are part of a minority group, there is often a definite discomfort about 'Where do I fit in here?' This also impacts on their base chakra. Many young adults whose families have migrated face this issue. The fact that some migrant families are conditioned to live and behave in the same way they did in their home country can affect their children's sense of belonging. It can create a split mentality, where the children do one thing with the family and another with friends. These kids feel torn between the world of their parents and their wider environment. It affects their ability to anchor their life, and know who they are.

I appreciate the difficulties migrant families face. They want a better life for themselves and their kids. But sometimes we don't realise the impact our attitudes and expectations have. I see the children of those migrants really struggling with the need to let go of the old ways so they can move on and fully integrate and embrace the freedom of choice that the new country interestingly had to offer their parents.

All these base-chakra issues can leave these kids feeling like they are in a state of limbo—wanting to be accepted in their family of origin, but feeling guilty for rebelling against their family. All of this adds weight to the inner struggle of 'Who am I?' and 'Where do I belong?' Many also speak of shame and bullying throughout their school years. It is heart rending. Displaced and confused, their constant worry of trying to fit in brings up feelings of unworthiness, rejection and of being unloved. Often they rebel as a way of trying to be heard within their family. If this falls on deaf ears it is not uncommon for these young adults to turn to alcohol, recreational drugs, inappropriate sexual behaviour, or become abusers themselves, in a world they make of their own.

These kids are the future. They reflect a global issue at the core of our humanity, as they define who they are in the world. By all appearances it is the same world as their parents', but this generation and future generations want to do things differently, and, because they are the future, we need to help them achieve this. Materialism will not necessarily sustain or be the mark of achievement for these young adults. There are many who are intent on finding and sustaining a greater sense of inner balance, peace, love and happiness that surpasses the material form.

23

You and your family

I find when dealing with base-chakra issues that one of the main themes to emerge is a person's right to be here, and how safe and secure their position is within their family. The right to be here on Earth is filtered through our childhood and adolescent experiences. Negative experiences impact on our ability to be grounded and function in a balanced way in our day-to-day life.

Each person handles their family circumstances in slightly different ways. What affects one person doesn't necessarily have the same impact on another. Most people I see are not grounded, and have scattered life-energy. Interestingly, after the session they comment on how they feel centred, light and back in their bodies. What they don't realise is that they are experiencing their body's response to their own life-energy when it's in balance. 'Take note of how you feel,' I say. The wonderful thing is that when your energy comes back into your body during a session, it is common to receive your own insights, giving you the much-needed clarity and direction you were desperate for.

There are a whole range of causes that can disrupt your base-chakra energy. As you read about these challenges you might like to explore some of the reasons why you may not feel comfortable in your body. These challenges range from parental survival issues at the time of pregnancy and after birth, to birth trauma, poor bonding with your mother, a major illness or some kind of trauma, and physical and sexual abuse, to name but a few. Taking recreational drugs, having emotional issues around trust and fear, fear of failure, personal expectations and expectations others have of you, family pressures, and cultural rules and secrets, also impact on your base chakra.

I often hear clients like Mark say, 'I just don't want to be here', 'I don't fit in', 'I feel different from my family, they don't understand me'. When these statements are made it is clear there are base-chakra issues and that the person lacks the basics in terms of security that help them thrive.

The building of security starts from birth. The base chakra reveals just how strong or otherwise your early foundations are in life. It speaks volumes about the family you were born into, and your early childhood experiences. How your family functioned and how you as a child dealt with family experiences become your foundations for adult life. There are many clues that indicate when your base chakra isn't operating as it should:

❀ When, out the corner of your eye, you witness a part of yourself floating or observe a shadow beside or behind you;

❀ When this feeling of isolation and disconnectedness to yourself and others is heightened;

❀ When there are paranoid or irrational feelings, or if you are aggressive or volatile or even racy or unable to sit still;
❀ When there's a fear that if you slow down you'll lose control;
❀ When you're oversensitive to noise around you.

Another indication that your base energy is not functioning properly can be when your nerves feel jangled as though you were living on the edge. There's often a feeling you're about to become unplugged if you're aware of your speech slowing down for no apparent reason, or when you're having difficulty with coordination, focus or self-discipline, particularly when doing mundane tasks. These can all be signs of poor base-chakra function. Another clue is having blurred vision, or feeling vague and spacey, a bit like when you've had a nasty shock. Feeling overly anxious, fussy, tired, fearful or lethargic, combined with a general sense of apathy can all hint at your base chakra not functioning correctly.

Being ungrounded for long periods of time *will* impact on your physical body. You may experience problems with your skeletal system and have lower back, bone, leg and feet issues. This may mean that in those areas you literally feel unsupported in your life. It may even manifest as eating disorders, or being generally rundown with frequent bouts of unwellness, because you're not getting what you need in life.

There are other tell-tale signs your base chakra needs help. You may recognise some of these:

❀ A pattern of trying to be successful out there in the world to gain Mum or Dad's approval, or trying to seek parental love through hard work and diligence;
❀ Trying to be successful for the good image of your parents, or finding yourself in a profession your parents would have liked to achieve.

Or perhaps you may find yourself living out a projection of Mum and Dad's unresolved fears and inadequacies by being successful in the world. This is a subtle issue that's nonetheless easy to take on board as your own. Often this situation isn't immediately obvious, but can still be loaded and packaged as love and approval.

In this chakra you can also harbour guilt around expressing gratitude for the opportunities and sacrifices your parents made for you as a child. This can leave you feeling that you may never be able to compensate for their generosity. When you have anger and resentment issues about the family tribe, this can lead you to rebel and alienate yourself from your family in an attempt to free you from familiar family patterns.

When your *will to live* in the base chakra is impaired, you are more susceptible to drug and alcohol addictions or sexual abuse. You're attracted to these things that help you feel adequate or in control. The problem is this only makes things worse, making your personal will weak and even less able to connect with your own personal identity.

It is a profound moment when you realise you have been unconsciously carrying around your mum and dad's patterns as your own.

You might prefer not to have to tackle base-chakra issues, as they are about the very foundations, or lack of foundations, in your life, but when you can let go your frustrations, past abuse, pent up anger and insecurities, then you start to experience an inner peace and freedom you've never felt before. Once you're centred and balanced in yourself and sure about what you want from life, clarity, personal vision and direction will follow. Your passion and zest for life will return. You'll feel like you've stepped into the flow of life-energy, instead of against it.

Nurture your foundations

The Australian Bush Flower Essence Boab combined with Sturt Desert Pea, Bottlebrush, Red Helmut Orchid and Fringed Violet are wonderful essences to help with releasing and transforming stuck family patterns that bind you to the past. More serious issues may need the help of a practitioner.

Areas of your body connected to the base chakra:
spine, coccyx, skeletal system, kidneys, hands and feet.

When your base chakra is working well:
you feel safe and secure in life.

Base-chakra issues will leave you:
worried about money, your work and/or the other basics of life.

Chakra colour:
red.

If your base chakra is out of balance you may be experiencing:

- Constipation, colitis, piles or diarrhoea
- Cold hands and feet
- Hip, leg and feet problems

- Frequent need to urinate
- High blood pressure.

Easy ways to nurture your base chakra:

- Walk barefoot at home and in the garden to help ground you.
- Dance around the house or join a dance group.
- Spend time around people who are supportive and make you feel safe.
- Try to walk in nature every day.
- If you're close to a beach, make time to have a swim.
- Cut down on your spending and put together a savings plan.
- Start to be aware of eating or not eating when you're upset.
- Eat red-coloured foods, such as apples, raspberries, strawberries and beetroot.
- Add some hot spicy food to your diet.
- Eat vegetables, such as potatoes and sweet potatoes, that are grown in the ground.

<h1 style="text-align:center">24</h1>

Sorting out sex, money, creativity and control issues

The first time I saw Florence she complained about pressure and discomfort in the back of her hip. She had already followed the normal channels of investigation, but had no answers.

Viewing Florence's energy prior to our session, I made some notes about each of her major chakras as part of my overall assessment. While each chakra is separate they are part of a continual interchange of energy that flows throughout your body, so I need to examine them individually and see how they are working together. Florence's base chakra appeared shattered, just like Mark's and the edges felt black and dark. It also appeared to be out of alignment with her other chakras. It tilted to the right, and there was a fluidic movement of astral/emotional matter dripping like a tap down to her feet.

Her life-energy was also contracted on both sides of her body. She looked as though she had been placed in a cylinder.

This told me that Florence was experiencing some major restrictions in her male and female energy and these were in turn impacting on her physically. This energy was holding her rigid, leaving her with no room to move.

From what Florence's energy was telling me she was in a very frustrating situation, with no sense of freedom or choice. She was a middle-aged lady who had done some work on herself previously. She now wanted to address her current issues before they completely overwhelmed her. One of the great benefits of working on yourself is that you become much more aware when something's not right and so are able to get help long before it impacts on your physical health.

When your life-energy is restricted your life feels restricted. This was Florence's situation.

Florence's sacral chakra appeared like a fuzzy line, like black splintered wood. It was elongated and the distorted energy had begun its stepping down process into her physical body, manifesting as hip pain. On her right-hand side towards the edge of her etheric body, I saw spiralling thought-forms randomly swirling in her emotional body, along with the piece of dead wood. A solid black egg shape also appeared in alignment with her sacral chakra.

As we discussed her life situation, she talked of feeling restricted, alienated and rejected by her peers at work. The distorted energy I observed on her right related to her male energy, making it hard for her to be assertive and forthright. We were on course. So, why was the energy on her left-hand side (female energy) contracted? It transpired this related to Florence's feelings of restriction, initially placed on her by her mother, where she never felt validated or heard.

When I started to listen to Florence's story I asked her about the events that happened in and around the ages of seven, nine, eleven, fifteen, seventeen, nineteen and twenty-one. These ages turned out to be key links connecting us to a timeline of critical life experiences. During these formative years, a series of situations had caused Florence to suppress her feelings, first in childhood, then adolescence and, as a result, in adulthood. Her life as a child had been tough. She'd faced the separation of her parents and sexual abuse. Then, as an adult, her marriage ended in divorce. This left her feeling angry, confused, exhausted and drained. She sat motionless in the chair in front of me, her eyes closed. There was a stillness in the room. Together we honoured her emerging feelings and mapped the energy she felt as it moved in and around her body, noticing where she had pain in her body. In the stillness Florence began to see certain patterns in her relationships, where she had not been heard. This left her with an overwhelming sense of frustration that undermined her ability to feel empowered.

Like all of us, everything we experience is stored in our cells as a pattern of energy that in turn colours our thoughts and actions. Florence could see how the past was now affecting her current situation, and as painful as her past experiences were, with this knowledge came awareness and growth. This meant that Florence was able to make different choices based on her new awareness. She had the right to speak up. Her energy started to come back, and finding the courage to change no longer felt so challenging. Florence felt a surge of clarity and vision that enabled her to focus on the now as she looked towards a positive future.

When dealing with the sacral chakra which governs how you relate to others, again you attract issues you haven't addressed. So, if you haven't worked on your self-confidence in relationships, then you'll continue to draw people and situations which mirror this back to you. If your base chakra (foundations) is not secure, this can create tremendous pressure on your sacral chakra (relationships, money, creativity, sexual function, etc.). One way of spotting sacral issues is when someone has volatile, emotionally manipulative behaviour. There will often be control issues in relationships, either controlling others, or being controlled. When there has been repeated abuse in relationships, the life-energy becomes distorted and can appear like a person carrying a colostomy bag, filled with dark, heavy toxic waste attached to the hip. All her life Florence felt controlled, and her hip was trying to tell her this loud and clear.

I have seen many sacral chakra distortions. Your energy may appear lopsided, displaced, disconnected, expanded, irregular, empty, toxic or torn and bleeding. It is not uncommon to see a break in the energy flowing between the base and sacral energies, which is a bit like having the power line cut to your telephone. It can also look like an old chastity belt, signifying an inability to have or enjoy sexual relationships.

Ruled by fear

Another image I see at the sacral chakra is a rubber ring just like a child wears at the beach. The ring, which is to keep something or someone afloat, tells me that they are experiencing difficulty with not drowning in their overwhelming emotions.

As the sacral chakra is connected to your emotions and the element of water, it describes the muddied boundaries you can hold close to the body, supposedly trying to keep you safe! If you have a ring of fear it tends to play out in all your relationships. You tend to attract a love interest with similar energy patterns or your fear from past failed relationships prevents you from stepping into new relationships, deeming them not safe. You don't trust anyone, and so that's what life delivers.

Not being heard

This chakra can hold the pattern of denial you experienced towards your childhood, adolescent or adult feelings. These unexpressed emotions can become crystallised, like an ice-cube, making it very hard to move beyond your sense of powerlessness, shame and guilt, or abuses from the past. Some people respond by withdrawing. Others are determined to be in control of every aspect of life, making a balanced approach to relationships difficult. Even abortions can leave an energetic imprint of the embryo's sac in a woman's womb after termination. In younger women I am finding an interesting correlation between the lack of personal power, abusive backgrounds, taking the pill and polycystic ovaries.

Sexual confusion

Confusion about your sexuality can also be a sacral issue. Abuse of sex, seductive manipulation, sexual acting out, sexual addiction, as well as obsessive attachments to people all compromise your ability to relate healthily. Sometimes sexual issues around physical and emotional intimacy are based on a desperate effort to feel and to have your needs met, so we end up confusing this desperation with love. This can be seen in women who have been rejected and abused by men in the past. Those who like to trade sex for power in relationships don't realise they're acting out of powerlessness, which hurts themselves and others. When working on these people, their energy can feel heavy, sticky and unpleasant, mirroring how they feel deep down. These issues often weigh down your aura to one side or the other, like a lopsided tent.

These are hard issues to tackle because they touch deep-seated pain. However, the bonus is that you get to taste what true love is. It's good to visualise other ways you could get your needs met, or what love would feel like in a nurtured healthy relationship. This will open the realm of possibilities to healthier choices in how you relate. Of course, as with all issues, you can overindulge or resist opportunities. So, sexually you may be frigid, cold or fearful, you could lack desire, passion or excitement, thus losing your drive, vim or vigour. Or you may be so compelled to have sex and find excitement so often that you wear yourself out, and then nothing seems to have much meaning.

The energy of trauma can create a heavy ring of fear around this chakra in relation to personal self-expression.

Lacklustre feelings

Another hint that our sacral energy isn't functioning properly is a feeling of emptiness or lack of life-energy. This makes your sacral chakra shrivel and contract, as does your life. This can be caused by excessive trauma, or by being worn down by an aggressive person or situation. Over time you stop feeling, so it no longer hurts. If you are facing sacral issues you will have a history of feeling helpless, hopeless or powerless in relationships. It is difficult for you to immerse yourself in life. You may describe yourself as feeling detached from your body. You might even talk of being somewhere else or 'off the planet'. You might be labelled a 'space cadet', living in some fantasy world you have created to cope with deep emotional pain.

When you have a balanced sacral chakra you are able to function with emotional intelligence in all your relationships. You are able to give and receive love, and to nurture in a balanced, healthy way. You are respectful of boundaries, your own boundaries and those of others. Feeling empowered and confident you don't need *to control* others through money, sex or in other ways as a substitute for your insecurities. You feel confident to explore and express your full creative potential.

Balancing your creative potential

The Australian Bush Flower Essences that are useful in dealing with relationship issues are Dagger Hakea, Five Corners, Flannel Flower, Gymea Lily, Boab, Bluebell and Red Suva Frangipani. Or you could use a relationship combination essence during times of deep intense transformation. Essences are like the guiding hand of a dear friend. They heal, support and soothe the mind and emotions during transitional times of grief, sadness and hurt. They are excellent when undergoing any personal development change or growth.

Areas of your body connected to the sacral chakra:
lower abdomen and reproductive area.

When your sacral chakra is working well:
life feels abundant, pleasurable, and you are able to enjoy your sexual self.

Sacral chakra issues will leave you:
unable to take pleasure in life or sex.

Chakra colour:
orange

If your sacral chakra is out of balance you may be experiencing:

- Perimenstrual problems
- Fibroids, endometriosis, ovarian cysts
- Irritable bowel syndrome
- Lower back pain
- Prostate and testicular issues.

Easy ways to nurture your sacral chakra:

- Eat orange-coloured foods, such as carrots and oranges.
- Be kind to yourself.
- Celebrate your achievements.
- Know you are a loveable person.
- Book an aromatherapy session or hot stone massage.
- Think about a dance class, such as belly dancing, that will allow you to express the joy of your sexual self.
- Have a long bath with scented oils and candles.
- Hire a clutch of romantic movies.

25

When you no longer know who you are

I grew up in a generation where children were seen and not heard. Parental authority and power over young children were a parent's means of control. Sadly, I can clearly remember hearing adults giving the advice to other parents that to gain control of a child you had to break their spirit a bit like breaking in a horse, so you could weaken their individual will. A well-parented child was good, quiet and submissive and never spoke back to their parents. Parenting success meant a well-behaved child who wouldn't have any difficulties fitting in to society. It was the way things were done back in the 1950s. Feelings, if you were allowed to express them, along with opinions and family secrets, were all neatly swept under the carpet. The strap, usually your dad's leather belt or Mum's hand, ruled the waves!

So, my brother and I grew up disempowered with lowered self-esteem, confidence and self-worth. He was bullied as a young lad, and I withdrew, becoming nervous and anxious. It was a struggle. I had difficulty in communicating openly and succinctly. Every word was weighed and measured for fear of a retaliatory response. Hence, it was difficult for the adult us to feel empowered. We didn't have a good sense of ourselves. This made it easier for others to impose their will upon us, which only served to further weaken our own will and identity.

My young daughter was playing at a friend's house one day and accidentally lost one of her Sri Lankan gold earrings, the ones we gave her on her adoption. I was disgruntled, disappointed and angry. *How dare she lose something that I was so attached to!* I remember calling her to the kitchen that day after I'd discovered the earring was missing. Angrily I blurted out in the heat of the moment, *the exact same words and negative phrases my mum had yelled at me as a small child.* I ranted and raved for what must have seemed like an eternity. What I vividly remember was the power of my feelings, and the intense need to assert my authority as a new mother over this little six-and-a-half-year-old. I wanted her to comply, surrender and admit shame for having lost her precious earring. What was I thinking?

Unconsciously, at the time I was trying to control her emotionally just like my mum had done to me. I stood frozen, shocked by what had just happened. *Where did that come from?* I sent my daughter to her bedroom and slumped down on the steps leading into the kitchen. I buried my face in my hands. 'Oh my God,' I kept saying over and over again. It was one of those highly charged moments, an unpleasant blast from the past.

Back then, though, I had no knowledge of family patterns, I found myself pondering my raw sweaty emotions. I felt sick to my stomach. I could feel the adrenalin rush as I tried frantically to search for some answers to what had just happened.

It was my first lesson in how unconscious issues can surface. It wasn't all that pleasant. This situation was a *huge* wake-up call for me. My behaviour in that instance appeared to be totally irrelevant to my daughter's early upbringing, and completely inappropriate when it came to my expectations of her, or at least that's what I thought back then.

I felt gratitude for the lesson to grow as a person and mother. In the coming days I continually reflected back on my early parenting skills as a young mum with two boys. I felt sadness. I smacked my eldest son far too often, even though I hated and resented this treatment as a child.

How easy it is to hand down a pattern of guilt, shame, values and powerlessness in a few brief seconds.

Too often we don't think about what we do each day. It becomes part of us. It feels normal. What you're exposed to as a child, you become emotionally and mentally wired to as an adult. This is such an important issue as it will be your knee-jerk response until you recognise what you're doing. Put your hand up if you've caught yourself speaking, reacting or responding in a challenged moment, from the wounded six- or nine-year-old inside? I have.

A great test to see how you're tracking is to notice how powerful you feel when you've been confronted. How do you feel about authority figures?

To finish my story, the earring could, of course, have been replaced. My daughter had little English at the time. I would like to believe that was my saving grace. Hmm! Does my daughter remember the incident twenty-five years later? Absolutely! She doesn't remember my words, but she does remember feeling shamed and being yelled at. She was fearful of my punishment. For her it had far-reaching consequences. As it turned out, I was also mirroring the angry, aggressive behaviour of her biological Sri Lankan father. It was hidden in the cells of her memory patterns as well. Learning that was yet another defining moment. The earring turned up a few days later at my friend's house. My daughter never wore it again.

Until I started to work on my own growth I was prey to unpredictable emotional outbursts, fuelled by a lack of personal control and a sense of powerlessness and injustice. As a child I learned material possessions were important. Everything needed to look good to make me feel OK about who I was. And now here I was projecting this very same pattern on to my daughter, all because I hadn't dealt with the personal powerlessness from my wounded identity housed in my solar plexus.

It takes a huge amount of energy to suppress an emotion.

So, what might my solar plexus energy have looked like as a child? I would say faint, withdrawn, sensitive and slightly toxic. I experienced a great deal of confusion about how I really felt. I lived outside my body. I distinctly remember thinking when the yelling got really bad at home, I felt safer in my head; no-one could see my thoughts or feelings. It was a survival tactic. As an adult, my solar plexus would have appeared overextended, exposed, possibly ripped or torn, a yellowish-brown colour from the build-up of toxic emotions. A healthy solar plexus is a beautiful, vibrant yellow, like sunshine. It is interesting to note that as a child I always had tummy upsets and abdominal cramps. I suffered with constipation, bloating, poor digestion and malabsorption. I had a lot of work to do to get myself back on track but it was worth it.

Each and every chakra is important, but as a practitioner I am constantly amazed at the number of clients with solar plexus issues. No doubt this has a great deal to do with the fact that so many of us lack a strong sense of identity and self-confidence in our lives. This chakra is the doorway to how you view yourself, your sense of personal power, spontaneity, confidence and self-esteem. That's why when you've had an argument with someone you sometimes feel as if you've been kicked in the gut. On an energetic level that's exactly what's happened.

Your solar plexus also represents your emotional power, and is connected to the nervous system and several other major organs in and around the stomach area. Your emotional intelligence and life experiences impact on the way your solar plexus chakra functions. Perhaps you've been trying too hard in life to prove your worth. Or you could simply feel emotionally drained, tired, shut down and cut off. When our solar plexus feels overwhelmed, we often need to withdraw. We can feel jaded, empty or depressed. Traumas and malfunctions of your solar plexus can leave you feeling low in energy due to suppressed anger and lack of self-esteem or confidence.

When we experience *emotional excesses* of anger, rage, depression, low self-esteem or self-worth, fear and so on, it drains our life-energy at the solar plexus. This lack of energy can show up as constipation, ulcers, irritable bowel syndrome, chronic fatigue, blood disorders, blood pressure, disorders of the pancreas, liver and gall bladder or eating disorders. A blockage to the solar plexus can also impact on your heart energy. If we become stuck in one particular chakra it impedes the natural flow of energy to all the other chakras above and below. When you lack a sense of emotional power and strength within, it may highlight an inability to feel comfortable with loving and nurturing yourself. It may also impact on your ability to openly give and receive love to those around you in an unconditional way.

Your own personal power barometer

What can you do about it? Allow five minutes for this exercise. Right here and right now, wherever you are, close your eyes and relax. When you feel calm and together, gently focus your awareness around the stomach, the area of your solar plexus chakra. Then, simply allow yourself to step back to a *difficult* time when you felt uncomfortable at home or work. Become aware of the *impact* your feelings had on you at that time. Repeat the same exercise but this time connect yourself to a *joyous* occasion. Generally, the first instance that comes to mind is the one your body wisdom wants you to notice.

Now, starting with your *difficult* time, *observe* your feelings. *Notice* the people you spoke to. Reflect on the conversation you were having at that time. Was it pleasant or unpleasant? Where did this situation happen? Was it in the home, workplace or a social setting? What did you find upsetting about the situation? How did it make you feel? Can you name the feeling, for example: sad, angry, lost, fearful or betrayed? Ask yourself, as a consequence of these feelings, how have they impacted and changed the way you think, feel, react or respond in relationships, work or generally today? This may be an energy clue to what is making you feel sick to the stomach right now.

When you are connecting with your *joyous* occasion, notice the words that come to mind. Are you experiencing happiness, joy, love, peace or calm? How positive or uplifted did this experience leave you? What has been a good outcome as a consequence of this joyous occasion? How did it change or alter your perception of life or people?

You can use this same exercise on any of the chakras. Stay curious and always open to viewing and discovering your internal landscape.

As we've already discussed, imbalances can be too much or not enough of something. The solar plexus energy can be very open, but not for the right reasons! Those who gossip and delight in repeating their personal dramas are hooked into everyone's emotional upheavals and are overusing their solar plexus chakra energy. Over time they will excessively stimulate, deplete or drain their own solar plexus energy, leading to health issues related to the organs found in this area of the body.

Your solar plexus chakra is also a psychic centre, so it's able to pick up on what's going on around you. That's the gut feeling you get that everything's not as it seems, even if things look great. Everyone is smiling at work, but you feel a little uneasy about the place, or you find yourself in an unexpected situation and are pleasantly surprised that you feel good about it. Your solar plexus can be a great friend in everyday life, helping you see beyond the obvious. To the budding clairvoyant, this can be difficult because you don't want to be picking up on everyone else's stuff. It can be like visiting a fun park's hall of mirrors—a little distorted.

When your solar plexus is sluggish you can feel like you're cut off from life and from your emotions. You can find it hard to see the wood for the trees because you can no longer sense your way forward. However, when you have good boundaries and self-identity, your solar plexus can reveal insightful information about people and places and your own emotional responses.

You can also drain your solar plexus by poor judgment, lack of trust in yourself, self-criticism, and a lack of will. You're basically giving your power away and meeting the world on empty. Encountering another person's energy field can also drain your energy. Some people are like energy-zapping vampires. Perhaps you can recall a situation where you've met someone, and after being with them for even a short while you felt tired and exhausted. I have. Have a think about the people in your life who have this effect on you. Once you know who they are you can be more careful about when and where you spend time with them. Getting together in nature is a great idea.

The solar plexus energy is felt, too, when you have those sinking feelings in the pit of your stomach, the nervous butterflies when you're anxious. This again is your early warning sign that things might not turn out as planned, which helps you rethink or tread with greater care.

The solar plexus is also that part of your chakra system where you meet and greet others in an energetic sense. Its sponge-like receptivity can form quick and strong reactions to other people and to your immediate environment. When you pick up on the vibes of a house, shop or workplace, your solar plexus is busy in action. Your solar plexus energy absorbs the vibes of those around you, sending important messages about what's going on in the outside world. When you lack boundaries and the ability to discern, your solar plexus can leave you feeling emotionally drained, sucked dry, unforgiving and compromised because the energy of the people, place or situation overwhelms you. If you have a balanced solar plexus they will be warm, effectively confident, have a good sense of humour and be able to meet life's challenges in an effervescent and positive light.

Support your emotional power

To assist the energy of this chakra, try these positive affirmations: 'When I honour and express my emotions in a positive way it is healing, rewarding and supportive'; 'Power is comfortable and safe'; 'Powerful people encourage me to empower myself'. The Bach Flower Remedies Larch, Honeysuckle, Cerato, Centaury and Crab Apple are wonderful when we need that extra boost of confidence in relation to this chakra. You could also try the Australian Bush Flower Essence Confid.

Areas of your body connected to the solar plexus chakra:
liver, gall bladder, stomach, spleen, pancreas, large intestine.

When your solar plexus chakra is in balance:
you will feel confident and optimistic.

Solar plexus chakra issues will leave you:
with low self-worth and feeling pessimistic.

Chakra colour:
yellow.

If your solar plexus chakra is out of balance you may be experiencing:

- Liver and pancreas problems
- Coeliac's disease (gluten intolerance)
- Gall stones
- Diabetes.

Easy ways to nurture your solar plexus chakra:

- Eat yellow foods, such as corn.
- Get outside into the sunshine.
- Spend time around those who appreciate you.
- Be more aware of negative self-talk.
- Replace this with a more positive outlook about yourself and where you're heading.
- Drink chamomile tea.

26

Getting the love thing right

Joan was a bubbly, vivacious, talkative lady in her mid sixties who had a love of all things beautiful. I listened with great empathy as she told me how she'd recently been diagnosed with breast cancer, but chose not to accept conventional medicine. Her decision was frustrating those close to her. I told Joan that I respected her choices. It was not my place to change her mind. She sighed with relief and settled back in her chair as I began to tell her what I had picked up in her aura. I spoke first about the huge veil of sadness that covered her face and throat area. She closed her eyes and, while I spoke, tears of sadness ran down her face. I asked whether she could relate to any of the words that came up like regret, remorse, confusion, loss and grief. I was trying to establish what was it that Joan didn't want to see. *What did she feel about herself that was so bad she deserved to die? Why was she mentally and emotionally punishing herself with thoughts of disgust and unworthiness? What was the reason she didn't deserve to live?*

Where the veil finished at her throat, the energy was jagged and cut. Joan had literally split herself in two, creating layer upon layer of suppressed fear and anxiety in her aura.

Now she was curious that I'd picked up so much. I continued. Joan's mask of having life under control slowly began to break down and she started to cry uncontrollably. It was such a relief—she hadn't cried since her diagnosis. Without realising it, Joan had heavily invested her time in settling her affairs—she wanted her family, partner and friends to remember her as a high flying, astute and successful business woman. She had prioritised her work responsibilities over the cost of her own life. Her need to be seen this way was obvious. Joan drew her ringing mobile from her bag. There were clearly no boundaries around work matters. To achieve this superwoman persona, Joan had hidden and suppressed the deep pain she carried in her heart.

As well, image and status were also important to her. Joan spoke about how her partner loved her feminine sexy ways and how she didn't look bad for her age. She felt important, loved and needed but went on to say the thought of having her breast mutilated or removed would be too difficult for her partner to cope with. How she looked to other people seemed to be more important than her will to survive. She said she would rather go out looking glam than bedraggled. Surgery didn't fit the image she had created of herself.

I was curious about why she thought her partner wouldn't cope. She told me he was a hard-working, blokey man's man who wouldn't know how to deal with the effects of breast cancer. I suggested she may be underestimating his abilities to be supportive. Joan felt she had him pegged. He was such a busy man and she was worried that her illness would bring their successful business to a grinding halt. She had worked very hard and didn't want to see it go down the tube! We looked at ways she could let go of some of her commitments, allowing for some peaceful, healing 'me time'—she deserved a well-earned rest.

It turned out Joan had been waging many battles for the business in the past two years, and she was beginning to feel the scars. Her driving force stemmed from long-term inner sadness and deep pain. Nineteen years earlier Joan had sent her three children to live with her parents. She had effectively abandoned them. The suppressed guilt and the feeling of being a bad mother ate away at her heart chakra. Around these hidden feelings Joan built a new world that while glamorous and impressive, masked a broken and sad heart. She went to enormous efforts to look good as a substitute for feeling good about herself. She invested a lot of personal energy in becoming a supportive care-giver to families involved in their business. Basically, her life was spent trying to keep people happy. Joan felt she was earning respect and a sense of worthiness with her helping hand and this, too, made her feel good about herself. But then this approach became too hard, giving her little to no satisfaction. It was now time for Joan to help herself.

In a loving and gentle way I asked Joan if she felt worthy to receive love. Her answer was, how could she? She had left her children, even though she had a barrage of good reasons why. This was the veil of sadness I saw covering her throat and heart chakra. This was the deep connection of pain to the lump I saw in the left breast, a dark hard lump of unexpressed grief.

Joan found deep relaxation and comfort in sharing her heart chakra pain. In our brief time together she laughed and cried. We worked on ways for her to forgive herself and to see the tumour as an expression of love. It was her inner self crying out for some attention. The years of self-loathing eventually became her disease. Like many of us, I could relate to elements of her story. Too often we try to make life great for everyone else and neglect ourselves. As with all her sessions, Joan brought me a gift of her honesty, I felt humble. I congratulated her for her bravery and courage. Joan eventually made a decision to start conventional treatment—and is doing well.

27

How you love

I see the heart chakra as the gateway to our love and passion for life. It is a *soulful* connection. By living the life you long for each day, you make choices that offer you love. Yet, too often you find yourself turning away, not feeling worthy to accept these gifts. How you have experienced love in your life can be the window through which you then view, express and create love in the here and now.

Self-acceptance plays a major role in the love stakes. If you don't accept who you are, you may limit your capacity for joyful, loving, happy and fulfilling relationships. Working with the law of attraction, if you hold a belief or attitude of unworthiness, you will attract people with similar belief patterns about love. By attracting these people who feel unworthy, you are never able to break the cycle and free yourself from relationships that wound the heart. Because we all so desperately want love in our lives, any past wounding of the heart chakra impacts on our health and wellbeing. Love is the glue that holds the universe together.

130

The heart chakra is connected to your *passion* for life—how you work, play and socialise. I'm sure you've heard yourself say, 'My heart's just not in it anymore'. How difficult is it to keep the home fires burning when we are drained of our passion? When passion fades it also drains your life-energy. Long-term denial of your passionate and loving self can lead to depression, disorders of the heart, immune deficiencies, lung and thymus issues, and even cancer. When you override your *feelings* it can feel like a part of you has died. And when you deny your passion and enthusiasm for life it can feel like you're on a downward spiral. It's a sign you've forgotten how to do what you love. Often you are so out of sync with your feelings that you are flummoxed. You don't know what it is you really *do* want, even though you don't like where you are. If this sounds familiar, it's time to take the journey home—back to your heart!

The heart has a connection to your foundations (base chakra) in life. If your trust has been violated or seriously abused you may feel fearful and wounded, making it difficult to access love and self-love. A first step towards understanding your heart is to look at your early years and your parents' love. Was it an open and affectionate love, or a closed doors kind of love? Was it gentle and loving, demanding or cruel? How did you *receive* your parents' love? Describe the way it felt to you without

When you deny your passion and enthusiasm for life it can feel like you're on a sinking ship! You simply have forgotten how to validate what it is that you care deeply about.

judging it. Write down the words that come to you—fun-loving, spontaneous, wacky, joyous, conditional, cold or absent. What do these words tell you about your attitudes to love?

If you had a loving mum and dad, love could feel warm and fuzzy, caring and nurturing. You may have felt safe and secure, especially around the home. If, however, your parents were violent, aggressive or angry, love might be equated with pain and abuse. If we had detached parents, love might be recognised as cold, aloof and distant. Sadly, not all experiences around love are perfect, but they do serve to influence how you might 'do love' and make different choices in your adult life. What type of love are you experiencing now?

My mum had a fiery *warrior-type* energy. This was the way she demonstrated and expressed love in the family. Her fiery nature wanted to be busy, always doing. It was a very physical expression of love. She demonstrated her love and care for me in a loud, forthright, domineering physical way. When I was in the early stages of parenting she would come around to our house and help dig up the garden, do the ironing, wash the dishes, all *very* helpful tasks when you have little ones. But I was a sensitive, watery, touchy-feely kind of person, and felt she was never able to love me as I wanted and needed to be loved: in a soft, gentle, cuddly way. I always felt emotionally vulnerable and wounded around her. I never appreciated her way of loving me while she was alive.

Because everything seemed like a waged battle, I viewed, labelled and typecast Mum as an insensitive, uncaring mother. Why? Because she didn't fit into my expectations and beliefs of what a mum should be like. Love was war, a bit like in the film *The War of the Roses*. You had to fight—after all she was a warrior! Love wasn't gentle.

The upside of warrior energy (when I wasn't being my sensitive, vulnerable, shy self) brought me an infectious kind of inspiration and stimulation, and gave me the motivation to move through some dark spaces. It was a heartfelt, tearful and forgiving moment many years after Mum's death when I was able to realise love comes in many different packages. The days of hard physical work she had given me had served me. They were her Xena-warrior-woman way of loving!

Love is connected to acceptance and forgiveness. When I managed to accept and forgive Mum, my heart began to let go of the pain, hurt and sadness from the past. The anger towards my mother began to melt like ice cream on a hot day. My heart felt like an open window, and the light of my soul was then able to flood my body. I was uplifted in a profound, magical way. Once I had moved from judgment to acceptance, forgiveness to understanding I could love Mum for who and what she was. This shift gave the adult me the power to love, accept and care for myself in a *responsible* way. It was an important lesson about perceptions being different from reality, and the many ways we read love.

When love has been absent in your life, you have a tendency to withdraw, to become cold, judgmental, critical and bitter. You set yourself up to be lonely and isolated. Fear of intimacy and relationships can become bigger than *Ben Hur*. Pain and trauma around heart chakra issues may leave you feeling rejected, abandoned or separate in some way. If you have been physically or sexually abused, the shame and guilt can feel like your heart has been torn apart, split or broken, because the energy to your heart chakra has closed down. That's your heart's way of dealing with painful experiences by shutting everything out. It can be difficult to trust people and situations, to believe good things can happen for you. Long-term grief can affect the heart on all levels, energetically speaking as well as physically. Unaddressed long-term emotional and mental issues, attitudes and beliefs that are connected to the heart, are a stepping stone towards all heart- and lung-related illnesses.

The things you need to focus on to heal your heart are self-discovery, reaching out, and any type of self-help therapy that feels safe. Emotional release and inner child work is brilliant. You might even like to try a simple affirmation around your worthiness to be loved. Say throughout the day, 'I am now worthy to be loved' and 'I am love'. Each day do something with the child inside that is nurturing, loving, playful and supportive. Buy some new clothes. Go to the movies, theatre or have a massage. Go surfing, play a game of golf or just take the time to lie on the beach without your mobile phone. Do something that you would normally consider a luxury.

As a practitioner I see the wounded heart chakra reveal its grief and trauma in many powerful images. I have seen spears, daggers, hooks and shotgun wounds in people's hearts. Some hearts have been oozing, open and weeping wounds, while others were small, shrivelled, withdrawn and walnut-shaped. Other hearts were shaped like a bomb about to explode, as brick or metal walls, as old gates, or surrounded by a moat. There have been hearts behind steel bars or buried down deep in wells. Many a heart I have seen is under lock and key. Though these images may sound strange, they are often the words clients use to describe the sensations they feel around their heart.

In energetic healing one of the most significant issues we deal with is the energy split that happens when the head is separated from the heart, or to put it another way: the physical body is divorced from the soul essence. When you move away from your heart's desire and passion, you are moving away from your soul's purpose. This is called a head/heart split, and it means you are living in your head, and have shut down the feeling nature of your heart in the way you relate to yourself and others. Clients talk about their frustration, confusion and drained energy, and how difficult it is to clarify the issues they are dealing with. Part of the purpose of energetic healing is to reconnect the head and heart energy, so that you can think and feel safely in your body. It is a common and grateful shift clients experience in a session when the healing energy of the head/heart comes together. By looking at their past relationships we can bring their *attention back* to their feeling in the here and now, allowing them the space and empathy to *feel* in a more conscious way. The sad thing is that today most people need permission to really feel what's going on for them, because they don't feel lovable, and because they live in their head.

One of the techniques used in energetic healing is focusing. You can do it yourself. Find a quiet space, perhaps you would like to light a candle or take the phone off the hook. Then take a moment to ask what is stopping you from receiving the love you deserve now in your life?

Focus your attention on your heart. Then breathe into your heart slowly, gently and lovingly. Imagine your heart opening like a rose or lotus blossom. Don't judge what you are sensing. Ask whether there is a message your heart has for you. This way you access your body's inner wisdom and intelligence. Be patient. Is there a word or colour that could describe what you are feeling or seeing right now? If it feels like a brick wall, for instance, how does this brick wall feel in your body? What does this brick wall mean to you? What area in your life are you blocking right now? If there is fear involved, ask yourself, 'What is so scary that I need a brick wall to protect me?' Remember, in focusing, awareness comes in small steps.

When you have established why you feel stuck, you can ask yourself, 'Is it time for this brick wall to be released now?' Yes? Then ask to clear all patterns around the need to protect your heart, to let go of the past pain and hurt. Using your mind's eye, place your heart in a cocoon of unconditional love. Send gratitude to your cell memory.

Great colours to use in healing around the heart are emerald green, pink, blue or gold. Choose one of these and see your heart bathed in this colour.

Focusing on an area of your body that feels blocked helps you to become aware of your energy and your emotional responses. And you can learn to access the memory in your cells. You can use this same technique anywhere in your body. The more you practise this simple technique the easier it will become. Learn to trust what you are sensing and feeling. It helps to build a strong communication link between your conscious mind and your cells' memory. Always allow time for the new energy to settle. Sometimes less is best. I often place an affirmation such as 'I am divine love' or 'I love, approve and forgive myself' at my heart after I have done this exercise. It helps support the shift in energy. Good luck and enjoy.

Discover your passion

Inspiring music can be a wonderful elixir to open the heart, as is following and doing something that you feel passionate about. Give yourself permission to find what makes your heart sing, if not today at least once a week. If you feel your heart is breaking, the Findhorn Flower Essence Heart Support has got me through many a difficult time. I use it either singularly or in combination with other essences for all my clients who have heart-related issues. The Australian Bush Flower Essences that are helpful are Hibbertia, Tall Yellow Top and Yellow Cowslip Orchid.

Areas of your body connected to the heart chakra:
heart, vagus nerve, thymus gland and circulatory system.

When your heart chakra is in balance:
life is loving, joyous, and peaceful.

Heart chakra issues will leave you:
unable to love, be generous towards others or to follow your passions.

Chakra colour:
green.

If your heart chakra is out of balance you may be experiencing:

- Immune diseases
- Allergies
- Breast cancer
- Heart problems.

Easy ways to nurture your heart chakra:

- Make a regular date to do something you love.
- Schedule regular time with those who inspire you.
- Follow your passions.
- Infuse everything you do with love.

- Read books and see films that are life-affirming.
- Spend time in nature.
- Be generous towards others—what you give out comes back to you.
- Eat leafy vegetables, such as spinach, and other green vegetables.
- Drink some green tea.

28

Finding your voice

As we journey up through our chakras, we begin to see how they're connected. Ben was a welcome sceptic to my line of work. He was born in an era when the mixing of religions was not readily accepted. Huge family rifts and damning words were heard down family corridors with those who broke with tradition, or married outside the family religion. Ben was one of those renegades.

It was his third visit. I was working on Ben's right-hand side near his sacral chakra (sex, money, relationships, control) when I became acutely sensitive to a strong older woman in spirit. It was Ben's grandmother on his father's side. It's not uncommon for me to be aware of a deceased mother, father, aunt, uncle or grandparents in a healing session. I was aware of Ben's disdain for other worldly experiences, so I chose to say nothing for the next twenty minutes.

When I felt the timing was right, I revealed to Ben that his grandmother was present. He burst into tears, and his story began to unfold. Because his father chose to marry outside the family religion, his grandmother saw Ben as a bastard child. His grandmother's attitude had a huge impact on his relationship with his mum and dad; he felt an absence of love and approval from them, too, and never felt noticed or validated. His family never gave him the right of his inheritance—to be here in the world.

Ben went on to describe his painful feelings of estrangement and of not fitting in that had plagued him at home, school and the wider world. A sense of worthlessness, and a feeling of being invisible, had begun in childhood and continued into his adult life. He had learned to shut down his feelings almost from birth, even though he wasn't aware of it.

As Ben spoke through his tears of pain, his body let go of the rigidity and tension it had been holding onto since he was a little boy. The destructive energy his cells had stored in their memory was being released.

This destructive energy that was frozen in Ben's sacral chakra and etched in his cells could be summed up in one word: bastard. Now this area was dealing with disease—Ben had been battling prostate cancer for ten years. And we were working with a raw pattern in Ben's life journey. He slowly began to release this sad cellular memory and his right leg jumped uncontrollably as a response to the trapped energy now being released.

This was a big moment for Ben. Over the years the unaddressed feelings and humiliation had slowly eaten away at him. And that's why he was always trying to prove his worth as a man. When he was a child he was never listened to or heard: he didn't have a voice (throat chakra). When he did try to assert himself by speaking up, he was simply disregarded.

While Ben continued to tell his story the tears flowed. I kept giving him permission to be here as I cradled his upper body, holding and gently rocking the hurt little boy who so needed a mum to tell him he was worthy to be loved. As the stored energy moved, shifting the distorted patterns he'd lived with for so long, Ben could finally feel alive, and be in his body. He was elated, amazed and grateful.

I sent him home to reflect on his beliefs and attitudes, along with the need to keep giving himself permission to be alive. Over the months that Ben and I saw each other, he spoke with a soft voice and gentle smile as we discussed his increasing awareness of his mind/body relationship. To date no other form of treatment had given him the inner peace he now felt.

In Ben's initial consultation when the patterns of pain had played out, he wasn't ready to address the feelings behind his situation. He was so angry and frustrated at the countless practitioners he had consulted over his disease. He kept saying they never listened to him, just as his parents never did. Now that had all changed.

Because of his early life Ben had escaped his desperate situation by living in his head. It was his way of coping with the pain. The straight dark energy line that I saw at his throat, combined with the contraction of energy on his left side, indicated that he had separated his head energy from his heart. He had also disconnected from his own spiritual aspirations, along with the ability to feel and receive love. He had not forgiven his grandmother or his parents for the pain they caused. There was so much resentment as well. Ben found it difficult to love himself and could only apply his love and devotion to his wife and children. When he came to see me he was at a crossroads: to continue doing for others or to find a balance between his commitments and honouring himself. Time was running out. Being a man of great responsibility, he was concerned for his family's financial welfare after his death, yet he yearned to go on a fishing trip around Australia with his wife. We looked at how he could bring those dreams into reality giving him the much-needed time to fish, relax and find inner peace, so deserving of such a beautiful man. Ben finished work and found a window of opportunity for part of those dreams to manifest.

Ben was an extremely intelligent, hard-working, sensitive and caring man, who cherished his wife and children. A wonderful father, he gave to his family what he would have liked to have experienced in his own childhood. In return, his family gave him the joy, love and happiness that was so lacking in his relationship with his parents and grandmother. Ben died twenty months later. Two months before he died, he wrote a short email thanking me for the work we had done. He said his gratitude would never be forgotten.

Not all healing we experience is in the body. In Ben's case, he finally found freedom from the terrible emotional pain he'd lived with for so long. I felt honoured that he had chosen to cross my path.

The throat chakra relates to the throat and neck region, voice and speech. This is an area I frequently see blocked or traumatised in some way. I see trauma in the throat area on people who have been abused, who lack a sense of personal power in relationships, or who have been bullied as a child. These abuses then make it difficult to speak up as an adult. They feel they have never been heard, as though they haven't a voice. This is a common complaint I hear.

Sometimes I see a straight line from the head to the torso, indicating an energy split, the separation of thoughts from the feeling responses of the heart. Horizontal dark lines can indicate a past life where a person was beheaded or guillotined. Some people have an elongated throat chakra, which suggests distorted communication due to lying, speaking in a malicious and vindictive way, or holding back important information. Not being heard by family, friends or work colleagues is another common story linked to the throat. This creates distorted energy patterns of closed, withdrawn, faint, blocked or cut energy at the throat chakra.

At the back of the throat, just below the base of the skull and in the etheric body, lies a psychic opening called the medulla oblongata. This area is connected to your breath, the breath of life, the sustaining life-energy that keeps us all alive and ticking. Breathing is the bridge between the mind and the body. The yogis and mystics of old placed so much importance on this area as a result.

So, in thinking about the health of your throat chakra, have you ever taken the time to check out how you breathe? Breathing helps us to connect to our physical body and our senses. As you read on, notice how you're breathing. Is it full and deep? Or, if you are anxious and tentative about life, is your breathing short and shallow? Just observe.

The second aspect of the throat chakra is divine inspiration. It can help spark your creativity and intuition. The knowing, like your sixth sense, is your *spiritual* perception. It is at your throat that your guidance from the unseen world connects with you, inspiring you to express yourself in wonderful new ways that are meaningful. This may be finding ways to give back if you are in business, beautiful new ways to present food if you run a restaurant, inspiring new colours if you are in fashion, or by just finding your groove. Whatever kind of expression is right for you can bring joy, hope and positive change to the world, uplifting you and those you come in contact with.

Though classified as a minor chakra, the alta major is located over the base of the skull. This area is linked to the throat chakra, blood pressure and body fluids. It provides a vital link to the third eye and crown chakra. These three chakras work together in unison, like cogs in a wheel, bringing about the stimulation and opening of your third eye, your symbolic and intuitive sight. The alta major is linked to your higher self, your soul.

Interestingly enough, I have noticed with clients who have been healers in previous lives, or involved in some type of white or black magic, that they have energetic scars that appear as dark crystallised blobs in and around the throat area. Often they were persecuted for their beliefs. Because our soul underpins the energy of the throat, the size, shape, colour and symbolic pictures I see around the throat area can look vastly different from person to person. This gives me clues as to how they are tracking in terms of expressing what is deeply or divinely important to them.

Distortions of the throat chakra can also be the result of surgery, vehicle or motorbike accidents, horse or whiplash injuries. The range and type of trauma is endless. Because the throat has a connection to the thyroid gland, bronchial tubes, lungs, voice and speech, those who suffer continual physical ailments linked to this area might like to ponder why these health issues are recurring. Do you often lose your voice or have a nagging cough? Do you have difficulty expressing yourself or speaking up? Perhaps you stutter or have a speech impediment. Or does the odd frog manage to croak in your throat regularly? When you speak up in large groups, does the skin around your throat get bright red and blotchy? All these situations can be a sign you have an energy block linked to the way you communicate and speak your truth.

Encouraging the client to share a time when their communication felt thwarted can spark a whole range of memories about when they thought it hard to communicate. Observing body language gives me more great clues. Notice what people do with their hands when they are talking. If they are constantly touching and trying to hide their neck, or playing with their tie, it suggests they aren't saying what the real issue is. Often their communication is simply not heard.

When there is a dark patch of energy over the throat chakra, but the client has had no illness, surgery or trauma to the area, I then look to the cellular memory of their past lives. There's always a fascinating story to be told. Chloe found it difficult to speak up and her throat chakra was withdrawn and small. As I studied her aura, I saw her energy was tipped to the right (masculine) side of her body. She felt separated from a part of herself, the left side (feminine) and her creative intuitive powers, but had no understanding why she felt this way. There had been no trauma to her throat in this life she was aware of.

There is a vital link between the throat and sacral chakra, so if you feel disempowered in relationships this too can affect your voice at the throat centre.

As we focused on Chloe's throat chakra she began to see herself as a battle-torn warrior in many past lives. She was angry about the injustices that had occurred during those times. This affected her ability to speak up and be heard in this life. Chloe still carried this strong assertive warrior energy in this life, but in an unbalanced way because the memory of those past lives had not yet been unlocked from her cellular memory. In a literal sense she attacked most things in an aggressive, assertive way, and struggled with the receptive intuitive nature of her own femininity. It was interesting to note that Chloe was constantly clearing her throat while she told me her story. As we released the cellular memory the ball and chain I saw at her sacral chakra began to dissolve, along with the dark black lump at her throat. Her male and female energy came back into balance. Chloe had felt held back and restricted all her life. Confusion she had experienced about her sexuality lifted. It was as though she had grown ten feet tall. She had a radiant beauty that was now reflected in her eyes. Even Chloe's voice changed when she spoke. It was softer, stronger and fuller.

The throat chakra is affected by not being heard, told not to speak, not to trust or not to feel.

The gift of being heard is a powerful gift of love from one human being to another. How have you felt when someone has taken the time to 'listen' attentively to you? Being heard is a *powerful* experience. It not only validates your feelings, but your right to exist!

When your throat chakra is working well, you feel strong and confident in all areas of self-expression and speech. You are able to pursue your creative endeavours with an inner knowing and trust that life supports you. You will have a connection to your intuition, and an ability to step into the rhythm and flow of life. You will be able to listen with empathy and compassion, and know that all is as it is meant to be.

Learn to speak your truth

The Australian Bush Flower Essences Bauhinia, Billy Goat Plum, Bush Gardenia, Dog Rose or Kangaroo Paw are excellent for those having communication difficulties of any kind. Affirmations to support the throat chakra are: 'I am now heard and rewarded'; 'I trust my divine self'.

Areas of your body connected to the throat chakra:
throat, thyroid gland, bronchial and vocal apparatus, lungs and alimentary canal.

When your throat chakra is in balance:
it's easy to express your feelings, to articulate your own ideas and beliefs, to feel heard.

Throat chakra issues will leave you:
unable to speak up about things that matter to you, unable to believe in your own creativity and feeling powerless around authority figures.

Chakra colour:
blue.

If your throat chakra health is out of balance you may be experiencing:

- Thyroid issues
- Mouth ulcers, tonsillitis, persistent sore throats
- Asthma and bronchitis
- Hearing problems
- Problems of the upper digestive system.

Easy ways to nurture your throat chakra:

- Sing in the shower and wherever you can.
- Chant your name with verve.
- Get creative.
- Enjoy what you create and have fun with it.
- Practice saying 'No' kindly, but firmly.
- Open up to people you trust.
- Practice being more confident around authority figures.

29

Second sight

Ethan was a thin almost ethereal-looking young man, quiet, intensely serious and constantly reflective, to the point that he was driving himself mad with his thoughts. He brought endless questions to our session. Ethan was a genuine seeker of truth and I admired him greatly; however, he had huge difficulty in trusting his own intuition, which in turn connects him with his truth. His childhood memories, coupled with his marijuana smoking, created a minefield of conflicting thoughts about himself and his life. He was angry with himself and his confusion, and worry and frustration left him physically and mentally exhausted. It was affecting his health. He felt weak, sad and depressed, and it was hard for him at work and play, and in relationships. He was constantly on the move, leaving people, places and countries due to his work commitments. This placed more strain on his already depleted nervous system. Not surprisingly, Ethan found it difficult to express joy and love in his life.

I found myself needing to encourage him continually to keep going, as he was so affected by his emotions. He had difficulty in speaking up, particularly around authority figures, and his voice was soft and ethereal, just like his overall energy. He couldn't stay grounded for long periods of time because of his own sense of self-loathing and disgust, coupled with his excessive worrying and mood swings. He literally didn't want the responsibility of being in his body, it was too painful. Ethan felt powerless on many levels and this affected his personal energy at the base, sacral and solar plexus chakras. His heart energy was also closed. I knew he genuinely wanted life to be different, as he had enrolled in classes to help him do this.

The dark hazy cloud I could see suspended over Ethan's third-eye chakra engulfed his head, making it difficult for him to get any clarity about the unhelpful patterns he kept repeating. His masculine energy on the right-hand side of his body was contracted and withdrawn. He spoke of a poor, insensitive father who never approved of or supported him. He felt emotionally abandoned. Ethan's belief was reflected in his own feelings and attitudes about himself. His childhood left him with low self-esteem causing him to feel separated from the strength of his own masculine energy. Basically, he was rejecting himself. This was evident in his poor digestion, irritable bowel syndrome and continually low energy levels.

To cope, Ethan found himself caught up in recreational drugs, which were also a contributing factor to his inability to be grounded. He found himself being overwhelmed by the illusion and fears of the *lower levels* of the astral plane. From these lower levels Ethan was constantly attracting more and more negativity. This made it difficult for him to connect with the strength and uniqueness of his own individuality. Because

Ethan couldn't stay grounded long enough to realistically deal with the demons from his past, he found himself caught up in a self-perpetuating vicious cycle, which only made his self-doubt worse. Each time he used drugs he fell deeper and deeper into despair about his life, losing motivation and will. He was giving away his personal power to the drugs because he no longer knew who he was. Ethan was continually seeing terrifying hallucinations.

Once Ethan stopped taking the drugs, started studying, meditating, cleared his energy field and committed to self-healing he was able to begin to turn his life around. As we went back through his past, he identified and released old crystallised patterns of pain that centred around his mistreatment as a child. It turned out that Ethan had been sexually and emotionally abused. Once his cells were no longer holding all that pain, his energy returned. This bought with it clarity and wisdom about his childhood experiences. He was then able to use his sensitivity more constructively. The wonderful thing is he now assists others with his insights and helps them with compassion and experience on their healing journeys. Using his intuition, Ethan amazed himself with his understanding and healing potential. He became an empathetic and sensitive practitioner who used the wisdom of his life experiences for the greater good.

Many people are fascinated by the whole concept of intuition and second sight. Often referred to as the third eye, the intuition chakra is frequently depicted by an all-seeing large eye, which hints at the mystical magic and insight it offers into life's greater mysteries. Located between your eyebrows and just above your eyes, your third eye connects you to your intuition, allowing you to see further than would otherwise be the case.

Some people are desperate to be psychic and foolishly set about trying to achieve this without any understanding of the powerful energy they are dealing with. In my field of work I find a lot of confusion between what is spiritual and what is psychic. Just because someone is psychic doesn't mean they're an advanced soul. Your life's blueprint or karma, your past and present life experiences, perceptions, beliefs and desires to progress as a soul, are influenced by the amount of work you've done on yourself to develop as a soul. Some very talented people I know are psychic and do brilliant clairvoyant work. You can be very psychic but not necessarily spiritual, as of course you can be very spiritual and not necessarily psychic.

Your third eye acts like an open and shut lens on a camera. How useful it is to you and how far it will develop depend on your intentions and on how much you assist others in life. If you simply want to be psychic or a psychic wonder, to get rich or to lead a fairly selfish life, then you'll never get the full benefit of the wisdom and perception of your third eye. Eventually you'll get lost in your own illusions, a bit like believing in your own publicity.

There are many ways you can harm your third eye's potential. So, instead of allowing it to help guide you through thick and thin, you will find yourself constantly making bad decisions. Drug use is bad news for the third eye. Abuse drugs and you may experience the kind of scary images associated with films like *Nightmare on Elm Street*. If you have experienced a major life shock or a bad accident, a rape, a mugging or such traumas, even traumatic past-life memories can close or open up your third eye unexpectedly. With this chakra you may find yourself totally confused, or get sudden blindingly and unnervingly accurate insights into what is going on around you.

Perhaps you were psychically gifted as a small child, but shut this window of insight because of a parent's disapproval. The shock of disapproval can cause you to distrust your instincts later in life. When the third eye isn't functioning properly it can feel like you're in a world of smoke and mirrors. If you get flashes of things that are bad and scary, that means your third eye is out of balance. The quality of your experiences depends on your development and wisdom as a person. If you are impressionable and tend to make poor decisions before your third eye opens, you won't suddenly be all-wise and all-knowing if and when it does.

When it comes to talking about the third eye in class, everyone is buzzing with excitement. It goes a little like this: 'Annie, when will my third eye open?' I reply 'Hmm, not sure.' My students continue. 'Will this class open my third eye?' I answer 'Maybe!' As they wait for my answers, often they are filled with disappointment. Like life itself, the third eye is filled with many possibilities, challenges and incredible timing. When we can appreciate and *respect* the magnitude of this chakra in our lives, and use it in a balanced, harmonious way, a powerful doorway will open. But you need to be patient. Right timing and caution are good things, as these opportunities carry responsibility in service, and the need to be careful of what you wish for.

You see, this chakra does hold many insights and keys to the unfolding soul and universal energies. However, it needs a solid foundation on which to ground its wisdom. Because your third eye links you with the universe and beyond, it is easy to get hooked into escapism by disappearing out of the here and now when life gets tough. The misuse or forced development of this chakra can lead to a paranoid personality and mental dysfunctions, so tread with care. For the energetic worker the insights this energy brings demand a good measure of humility, empathy, compassion and *increased responsibility* if it is to work for you.

When your third eye is abused you can become a victim of obsessions, nightmares and visions. Those who force their third eye open are then unable to switch off the barrage of thoughts and images from daily life. They may even be plagued by the spirits of those who have passed over. To avoid confusion with the energy of this chakra you need to discern whether the messages you are receiving are coming from your solar plexus (lower mind and past patterns) or the higher vibration of your soul's intuition.

Being psychic is not only associated with the third eye but also with the solar plexus or gut instinct. Intuition is a more profound knowing, based on the love-wisdom connected to the third eye. It is a higher vibration than the gut (survival) instinct. The funny thing about the knowing and seeing connected to the third eye is that it's an *inner* knowing and seeing, an inspired insight when you least expect it. This inspired understanding can often happen at 2–3 am or on rising. Just as it can when taking your shower, watching television or sitting on the toilet.

When my third eye began to open it was a curious and exciting time. My guide managed to pop into my mind's eye while I was making my bed! It was as clear as the picture on a television screen and totally unexpected. I gasped! My guide's image was that of a smiling dark-skinned man with loving sparkling eyes, dressed in the brown robe of a monk. His face was unfamiliar, but his love-filled eyes caught my attention, along with his humorous cheeky grin. I found myself smiling back in that *split second*. Was I going mad? I laughed at the thought of having a vision when simply making a bed. Sometimes we can try too hard to have these kinds of experiences, blocking possibilities and frustrating ourselves. The third eye is very spontaneous. This energy moves very quickly because it is vibrating at high speeds. Focus too hard and you'll lose it. Prior to my vision, I'd been meditating and writing in my spiritual journal.

Connecting in this way to the unseen spirit world can fill you with a sense of life's magic and love. After my vision I felt this illuminating buzz of excitement, happiness and satisfaction, switched on like electricity. I bubbled over with joy for the rest of that day. When you have positive experiences with your intuition, and begin to trust it, your intuition responses grow. It's like developing your spiritual muscle. The more you learn to *trust* your intuition, the more you empower yourself to let go of the need for others to tell you what you should or shouldn't do. You switch on your deep knowing, accessing greater clarity, truth and wisdom. When your third eye, your sixth chakra, is working well, you'll trust your intuitive perceptions and symbolic messages. Your memory, recall and visualisation will be strengthened, and so you will be able to see further than most.

Discover the great mysteries of life

When you're having difficulty being grounded or have that spaced-out feeling, I suggest you try the Australian Bush Flower Essences Bush Fuchsia, Crowea, Red Lily, Sundew or Fringed Violet. When there has been sexual abuse Flannel Flower, Wisteria and Fringed Violet are excellent. The above essences combined with any type of energy healing can bring about a swift and significant shift in people who want effective change or growth in their lives. A great affirmation is 'I now see clearly'.

Areas of your body connected to the third-eye chakra:
thyroid, parathyroid, reproductive organs, adrenals, pancreas, brow, left eye, ears, nose and nervous system.

When your third eye is in balance:
it's not difficult to be imaginative and intuitive, to think clearly and make good decisions.

Third-eye chakra issues will leave you:
confused, suffering tunnel vision, and unable to intuit what's best for you.

Chakra colour:
indigo.

If your third-eye chakra is out of balance you may be experiencing:

- Migraines and tension headaches
- Eye defects
- Catarrh and sinus issues
- Ear problems.

Easy ways to nurture your third-eye chakra:

- Start to listen to your own inner wisdom around everyday issues.
- Become more aware of the vibes around you.
- Learn tarot to boost your intuition.
- Give yourself a pat on the back every time you intuit something correctly.
- Begin to take note of the nuances in conversations, in the energy around yourself and others.

30
Mind games

Louise asked me to look at the energy around her head and in her brain. As I was scanning this part of her aura I noticed what looked like one electrical wire in a network of wires (like the nervous system) had fused! 'Hmm!' she replied, when I told her what I had seen. Unbeknown to me, Louise was undergoing tests for epilepsy or a possible brain tumour. Fortunately, she had neither. I asked her what had she been thinking about constantly. What was she worried about? What had she been trying to *think* her way through?

Louise admitted that her mind was going in many directions because she had several pressing issues she was trying to resolve. And she was mentally exhausted as a result. In a way she had *blown* a mental light bulb. Her brain felt like it was swollen and her head actually hurt. When she took the time out to tell me what was going on in her head, Louise quickly realised how I had seen what I had. We both laughed. This situation helped her see how she deals with stress, and what impact it has on her mentally. It's like when you open too many windows on your computer: it crashes! Your crown energy on the top of your head is like a receiving station. When overloaded, it can simply shut down leaving you feeling burnt out. This is an increasing issue for all of us in twenty-first century life. Sometimes it's like you're hardly in your body at all. Louise's mind was in overdrive, so she became frazzled. Interestingly, the medical tests revealed a variation in her brain waves, but were unable to establish a cause.

By contrast, when Matt walked in, he had the most golden light in an aura I had seen for some time. A man like this would look back at life with little regret. He had been meditating for years, had done plenty of work on himself and lived with ease and grace. His crown chakra was extremely open and operating well. I sensed strongly that Matt had already glimpsed the beauty of his spirit. The light around him was luminous, and appeared to flow effortlessly down the right-hand side of his body.

However, I was initially confused as to why only one side of his aura appeared to be bathed in light. I was looking forward to our session to find out. I moved my attention from the subtle bodies of his aura to his chakras for some more clues. Therein lay my answer. Matt had wonderful incoming crown energy, but all this beautiful life-energy appeared to hit a roadblock when it reached his third-eye chakra. From here it moved sideways down the right-hand side of his aura. For some reason his third eye was veiled.

Matt was not allowing himself to see the truth of who he was, or for that matter others either. Because his energy wasn't being grounded through his body, it was like one side of a tent flapping in the breeze. All his wonderful golden life-energy was being dissipated. I was sensing a *resistance* to Matt's soul being aligned with his everyday personality. When I looked further, I could see he had not addressed his family and relationship issues (base and sacral chakras). Also, he didn't feel pure enough to accept what a special soul he was. Matt told me he wasn't comfortable with the word 'God' because it had 'too many religious connotations', though he did sense there was a cosmic spirit in life.

As Matt's energy was contracted and withdrawn on the left side (feminine/maternal/mother) of his body, I could see there would be a story to tell about his mum. In fact, there was a line of energy sweeping down from the top of his head (crown chakra) moving like a swirling 'S' through his aura. It crossed his body from right to left as it tried to ground the light of his soul through his left foot. Matt was aware, in a responsible way, of the light he carried, but he had a tendency to compartmentalise his feelings. He liked life to be divided into neat little boxes, and this is where he was coming unstuck. He felt he was losing control and falling back into old patterns. It turned out he was in a new relationship and his partner was struggling with the same issues. He understood that his partner was mirroring his issues, which is often the case, but felt powerless to change them. It turned out that we were dealing with some crystallised attitudes from several past lives where he had difficulty committing to relationships, coupled with many ascetic lives lived in monasteries. Once recognised, he remembered it was all too familiar to him.

Together we then weaved our way back through this life to seven years previously when his trust in himself was shattered after a relationship break-up. We spoke about his perceptions of his mother and how this may relate to his contracted feminine (left side) energy. Matt told me his mother found it difficult to receive, feel, touch or love and that she had a bit of a stiff-upper-lip attitude. While he spoke he realised he had taken on this pattern, and was not giving himself love, warmth or acceptance. He also attracted this by choosing women in his life who kept leaving because they wanted to stand alone.

We did some further work on the past and discovered that when he was three his mum and dad left for a holiday leaving him to be minded at home. Matt was inconsolable, so his parents returned immediately. This sense of abandonment went deeper. Matt went back to a time before and during birth when he felt the despair of coming to Earth and his spirit being imprisoned in his tiny body. In a funny sort of way he was angry with God. He was punishing God and himself, because he didn't want to be here. Matt was holding himself back, he was a reluctant participant in the game of life. The irony was that with such a strong crown chakra, he had a lot going for him. Once he had put all the pieces of his jigsaw together in the session, he left feeling the power of his energy flowing through his body. Matt left with gratitude, knowing the steps he needed to take within for further and ongoing healing.

31
Soulfulness

Your crown chakra has many names that describe the type of energy it taps into. It is your connection to your life force: *God, Creator, divinity, the universe.* Whatever label works for you, the energy *source* is the same. To establish a healthy relationship with your crown energy, you need to be open to the divine aspect of life. This is not the same as being religious; it's a deeper awareness that feeds your spirit. As you read this chapter, you may discover whether your crown energy has been opened or perhaps why it remains closed.

While some derive great comfort in seeing God as the source of all life, those without specific religious beliefs don't find this helpful. Over the years I have found that the word 'God' taps into our hidden thoughts, emotions and agendas that haven't yet been addressed about spiritual potential. The word 'God' can evoke anger, guilt or the need to be in control. Take a minute to notice your *reactions, responses and associations* to the above words. Say each word aloud, then follow it with a reflective moment. How does each word feel in your body? See which word has the least favourable response for you. Ask your soul who or what has influenced these feelings. Wait a few minutes, then ask your soul what your understanding is now. As you examine your responses, see how your own thoughts and beliefs could be stopping your connection with the life source—because ultimately that's what we're talking about. Continuing on, based on your thoughts, take another moment to ask, 'How have I perhaps stopped the flow of this divine energy through my crown chakra?' Are you harbouring past resentment, anger or unworthiness about your wonderful unique self and the many gifts you have brought here? To shed further light on possible issues, take a look at your family's history of associations with soulful subjects. You may have inherited unhelpful beliefs.

When you aspire to be one with the source of all life, you open yourself up to a well of endless divine inspiration. Your spiritual aspirations, devotion, prayer, meditation and interest in spiritual subjects helps draw this powerful life-energy to you, and helps open your crown chakra, your direct line to all the things that will feed your spirit. This chakra is your pathway to your inner wealth and higher power. When this connection has been opened, you will notice a blissful feeling of expansion, fullness, emptiness and nothingness all at once. You may also feel heightened awareness, deep happiness and joy. This love *feels* all-embracing. You may even experience a letting go of the fear of death, or aspects of life that have held you back. Words are inadequate to describe these and other unique soulful experiences that can be yours. You may hanker to recreate these moments but can't. We call these moments peak experiences. It is a glimpse into *who* you really are, the divine you that is connected to *all* life.

These moments allow you to see life with crystal clarity for a short period. Here you experience an expanded version of your little self (personality). You sense nothing is impossible. The energy that flows from the crown is connected to your life purpose in the deepest sense. It is your connection to a higher power that is *limitless*. When this centre opens, you are in direct communion with your higher self/soul energy. It's a place of profound acceptance, understanding and peace, way beyond your physical self. It's big picture stuff!

Connecting back to previous chapters about you and your family and your base chakra, when clients say they don't fit in or relate to their family of origin, it's as if their birth saw them land at the wrong airport! Well, once the crown energy has been expanded, these old beliefs and attitudes become obsolete because they taste true and profound belonging. Love is the glue that holds the universe together. You don't need anyone to tell you this when your crown chakra is open, you *feel* this in every part of your being.

There are many reasons why your crown energy can be closed or temporarily blocked. These include not *being open* to your spiritual self, to learning, to understanding, to knowledge and education, to listening, or to your beliefs about life. Spiritual experiences and knowledge are limitless. They don't fit the tiny little boxes that you may want to put them in. I'm sure you've all heard people say, 'Oh, so and so is *so* closed'.

> *Its helpful to know that your soul likes to talk to you through symbols, as these can convey so much more than words.*

They may be speaking figuratively, but in fact this is what we do energetically.

When I see a large cloud sitting above or to one side of someone's head it can suggest depression or fear and confusion. I often see electrified and frazzled hair around a person's head, as if they have stuck their fingers in an electrical socket. This can represent burnt-out mind energy due to over-thinking. Louise's story demonstrates this beautifully with the symbol of a burnt-out wire in her electricity meter box! This is a common sight around students, especially at exam times when they try to cram information.

People who spend a lot of time trying to work things out in their head and disregard their feelings can have a blocked crown chakra. The overanxious, analytical thinker who never gives his mind a break is in the same boat! Sometimes this can be as a result of a lack of faith that the universe will support you, or you may have rigid belief patterns or be cynical about spiritual views. Or you might be someone who has a powerful mind and dominating will, or you may have chosen denial as a way of coping with deep mental or emotional pain.

Long-term depression, nervous and mental disorders, schizophrenia and the taking of recreational drugs all impact on crown energy. Those who suffer from migraines, headaches, frequent accidents or have had surgery to the head may also have blocked crown chakra energy. The crown chakra is another site where I often find energy cords attached. These dark threads are similar to guy ropes on a tent. They tell me this person is being held down or back by the overuse of their masculine or feminine energy. When there is a head/body *energy split*, as discussed in earlier chapters, it blocks your spiritual awareness because the links between the mind (head) and heart (body) have been temporarily unplugged.

Where the client presents with powerful energy distortions to the head there will be little to no energy at their base chakra. They often feel like they are falling or tripping over, or find it difficult to slow down because they're not balanced or centred. When there has been substance abuse—recreational drugs or alcohol, particularly binge drinking—corded attachments to the crown chakra drain the person's energy, literally sucking them dry.

These clients often say things like: 'I just can't think straight', 'I am easily distracted and keep losing it when I'm talking', 'This will sound weird, but I feel as if someone is playing with or in my head', 'It's as though the light has gone out', 'I feel completely disconnected from my body', 'Sometimes there is this weird sense of pressure on the top of my head' or 'It is like someone is trying to pull me out of my body'. If this has happened to you, it can be a very scary and fearful experience.

Another common energy pattern connected to the crown chakra is that of a vertical line like a car aerial used to pick up a signal or radio frequency coming from the top of a person's head. This tells me if they have a strong connection to their divine self. The colour of this vertical line tells me whether they are picking up on unhelpful (black) or positive (gold) frequencies. Unhelpful frequencies will give you the impression of being out of tune with the flow of life-energy.

The session has the opportunity to reach its greatest healing potential when the client is open to receive.

If this is the case daily life can be painful and frustrating or you may experience persistent headaches.

When your crown chakra is balanced and active, you have a thoughtful and open mind to perceive, analyse and assimilate information. You are aware of the greater plan of universal life. You have the ability to connect with your spiritual wisdom and identity. Life flows. Instead of having to plan or control every aspect of your life, there's room for little miracles and synchronicities. You know intuitively the best direction to take. While life still has its moments you feel blessed, and your presence is a blessing to others. You light up the world.

Open up to your spirit

A great old Tibetan mantra that helps to align your personality with your soul energy is: 'I am the soul, I am the light divine, I am love, I am will, I am perfect in my design' or simply, 'I am one with my divine essence'. A few of the Australian Bush Flower Essences that can assist in this process are Angelsword, Mint Bush, Red Lily, Black-eyed Susan, Boab, Bush Iris and Bush Fuschia. A combination Meditation Essence is also available.

Areas of your body connected to the crown chakra:
pineal gland, upper brain and right eye.

When your crown chakra is in balance:
the whole world seems beautiful. You feel connected to yourself, to everything. Life is pure bliss.

Crown chakra issues will leave you:

with a head full of thoughts, disconnected from your spirit and from the world around you.

Chakra colour:

violet.

If your crown chakra is out of balance you may be experiencing:

- Mental health issues
- Dementia
- Confusion
- Dizziness
- Depression.

Easy ways to nurture your crown chakra:

- Learn to meditate.
- Spend a little time each week doing things that make your soul sing.
- Read inspirational books.
- Collect DVDs that lift your spirit.
- Add grapes, blueberries and other purple foods to your diet.
- Burn lavender oil.
- Find a little quiet time each day to come back into balance.
- Turn off the car radio and immerse yourself in a little silence.
- Take an interest in spiritual teachings.

32
Pathways of light

The first window into what's going on in your life is through your aura. The second is through your chakras. The third is through the meridians: beautiful webs of light and life-energy that weave through your body like a winding road with a million junction points. Our understanding of the meridian system is based on information that's been gathered for over six thousand years by ancient Chinese practitioners. These meridians connect your internal organs, subtle bodies and chakras.

Traditional Chinese medicine looks at a miniature version of the whole: our universe as the macrocosm and human beings as the microcosm. Put another way, we mirror the universe we live in, as everything is connected. For each action there is a reaction that impacts on the people, places and situations around it.

Throughout creation there is a constant flow of life-energy. To merge with this flow of life, you need to live in harmony with nature so that you can experience its natural rhythms. We see these rhythms in the movement of the seasons, and the cycles of the sun and moon and tides. The source of life-energy—chi, as the Chinese call it—comes from air and food, from the experience of love and touch, from stimulation and impressions. This precious life-energy flows to every organ and every part of your body. When your environment, lifestyle or emotions overwhelm you, your chi can't flow, so you become sick. Disease tells you that everything's not well inside, and your thoughts and beliefs can then block the healing process.

Every person has twelve meridians that run along either side of the body. Two other meridians, called the conception and governing vessels, only have one channel that runs down the midsection of the front (conception) and back (governing) of the body. Each meridian is divided up into positive and negative life-energy, which travels up and down and in and around the body. We know this energy as yin and yang. Yin embodies the feminine, restful and nurturing qualities, while yang includes the masculine qualities of action, heat and movement.

The yin and yang qualities represent different parts of your body. The inside of the body is related to yang, the outside surface is yin; the back is yang, the front is yin. Some organs are yin and some yang. Even the day is divided into yang (morning) and yin (evening).

Yin and yang are meant to be in balance, but most of us tend to have more of one quality than the other and need to work on the balance. Where do you think your leanings may be? What qualities do you need more of in your day—at home, at work, in relationships—to come into balance? Do you need more rest, more time for reflection or to get moving a little more? How can you introduce this in simple steps into your routine?

Jorgen Frydenlund, a Danish oriental medicine practitioner, tells us in his book *Understanding Meridians* that: 'yin and yang are mutually attracted to each other, the purpose of which is to maintain or to restore balance'. A person can be seen as more yin in qualities than yang, therefore requiring stimulation of their opposite qualities to bring them into a balanced state.

Each meridian shares a partnership with another meridian in this intricate system. The partner meridians are like cousins because the energy works together, like part of an extended family. If the life-energy is disrupted or affected or out of balance in any way, the partner meridian will be affected too (see Figure 3, Partner and cousin meridians).

The Yin energy flows from the feet to the head, whereas the Yang energy flows from the head to the feet.

Each of the meridians starts or finishes at the feet or hands, and the energy flowing up and down these pathways acts as communication circuits between the physical and non-physical (aura and chakra) parts of your body.

In energy healing, when there is a problem with the fingers or toes we look at the corresponding pathway to give us a clue about where the energy might be stuck. See Figure 2, Fingers and toes, below. Have you had any problems with any of these body parts? A little further on we'll see what thought or emotion the meridians correspond to.

If you go to an acupuncturist you will find them taking your pulse to gauge the flow of blood moving through your veins. They'll describe this flow of blood throughout your body as heavy, floating, stagnant, deficient or even collapsed. These

Figure 3: Partner and cousin meridians

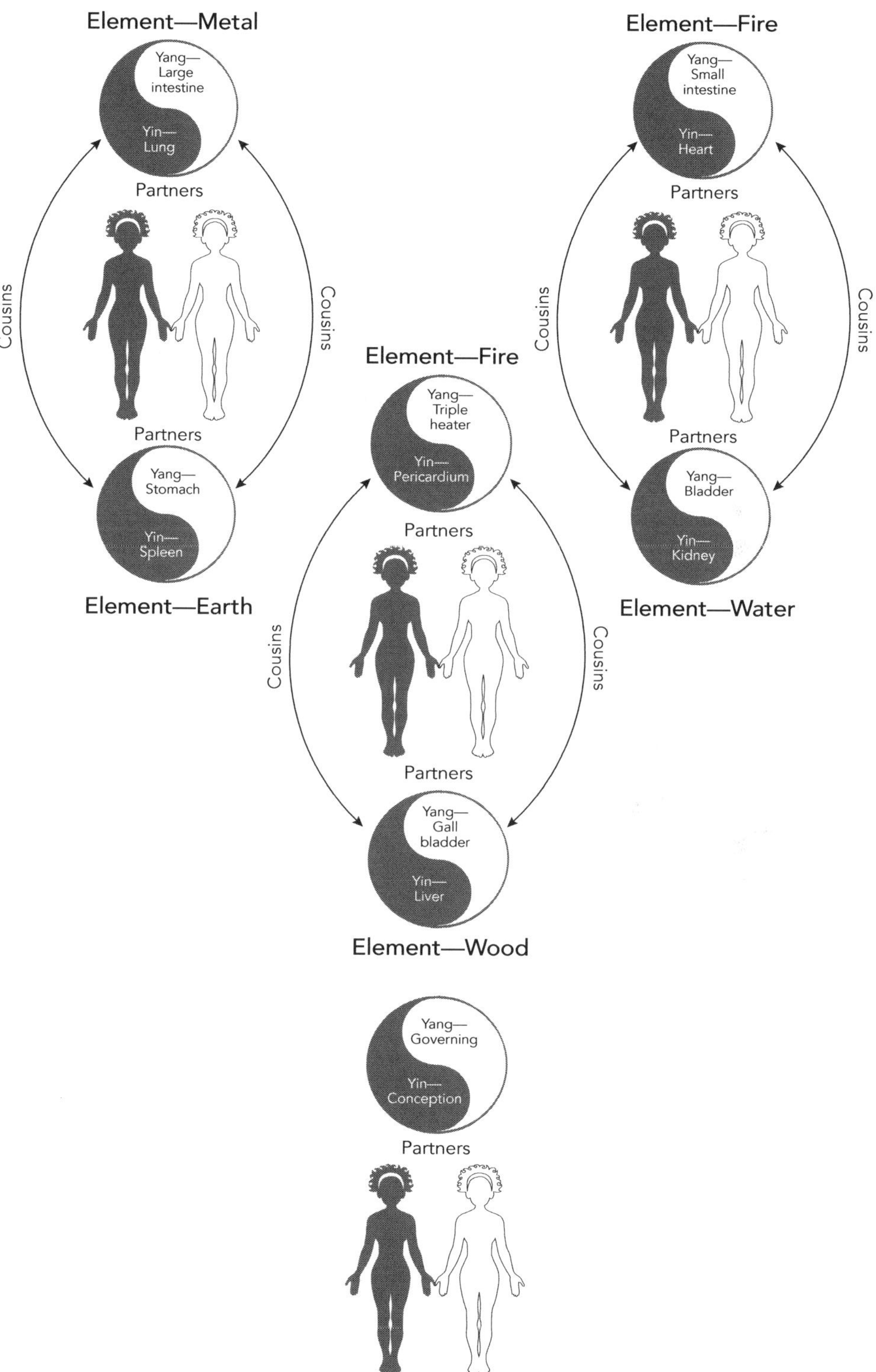

Yin qualities: feminine, receptive, nurturing, cooling, holding and resting
Yang qualities: masculine, dominant, action, movement, transformation and heat

Figure 4: Fingers and toes

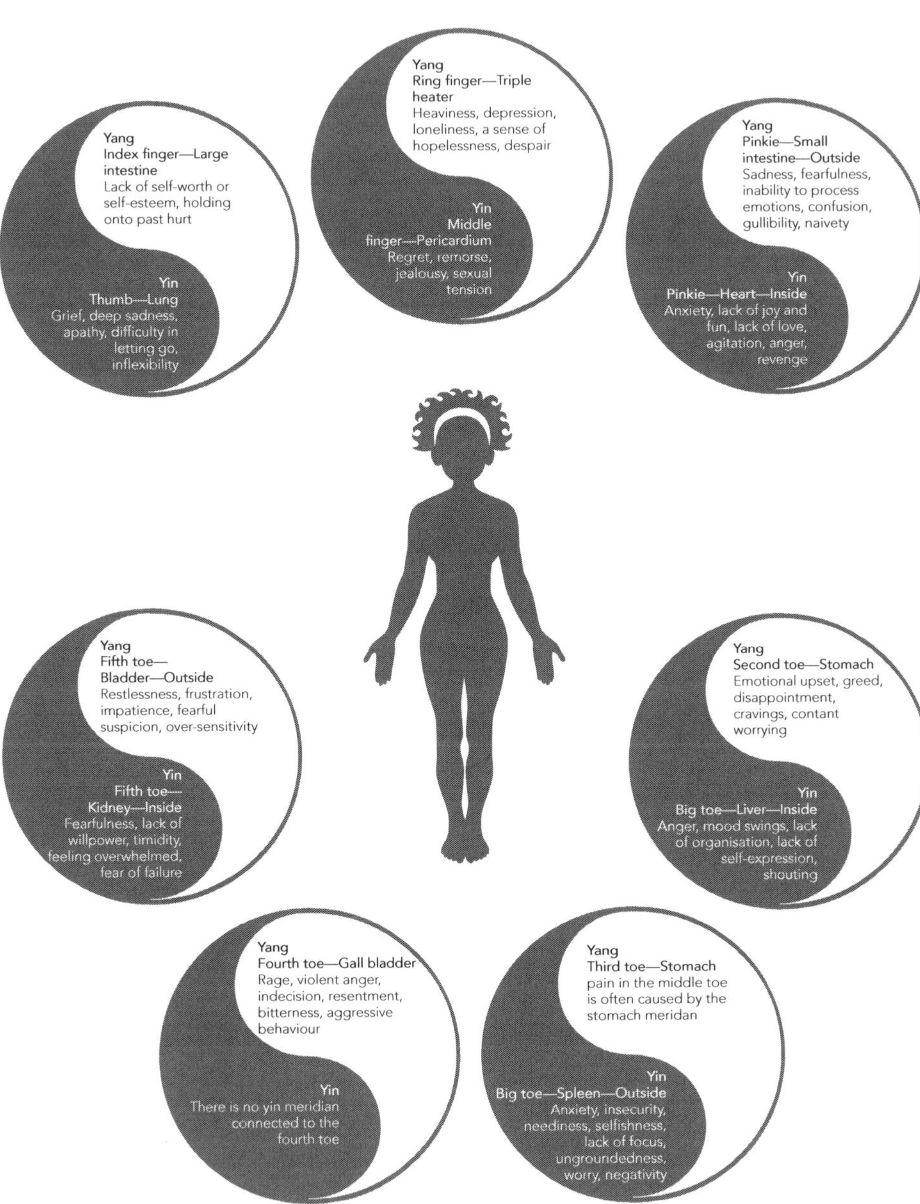

words indicate the *quality* of energy supply to each of your organs, as well as to the corresponding meridians. Your blood is considered to be yin. The heart rules the blood.

Along your meridian pathways are tiny little connection points that run between the body's organs and muscles. These points are where the acupuncturist will place a needle to stimulate and support a meridian's movement and the flow of life-energy. There are approximately five hundred of these small points throughout your entire meridian system.

By contrast, the energetic healer will muscle test, sense or feel your energy, or use a pendulum to find imbalances in your meridian flow. Working with their hands, the healer may brush the meridians in the etheric body of your aura, or pulse and hold various points along your meridian pathways. This does a similar job to the acupuncturist's needle, stimulating the flow of life-energy through the meridians' intricate pathways.

Meridians exist inside and outside your body. When you are sensing and tuning into the meridians, they can feel cold, floating, tingling, slippery, drained, open or closed.

So, what does all this mean in your daily life? Bella complained of extreme tiredness and lethargy. She felt drained and despondent, and suffered from poor digestion, bloating and constipation. She had spasmodic pain and discomfort in her stomach as well. Bella's pulse felt empty and faint and her skin appeared to be pale and dull. She spoke about recent difficulties in the workplace. Her relationships with her co-workers were at an all-time low and were a major cause of her worry. Bella also lacked confidence in her work skills. She complained about unusual spasms in her big toe and an itchy left thumb, commenting that it probably wasn't related at all to her current situation.

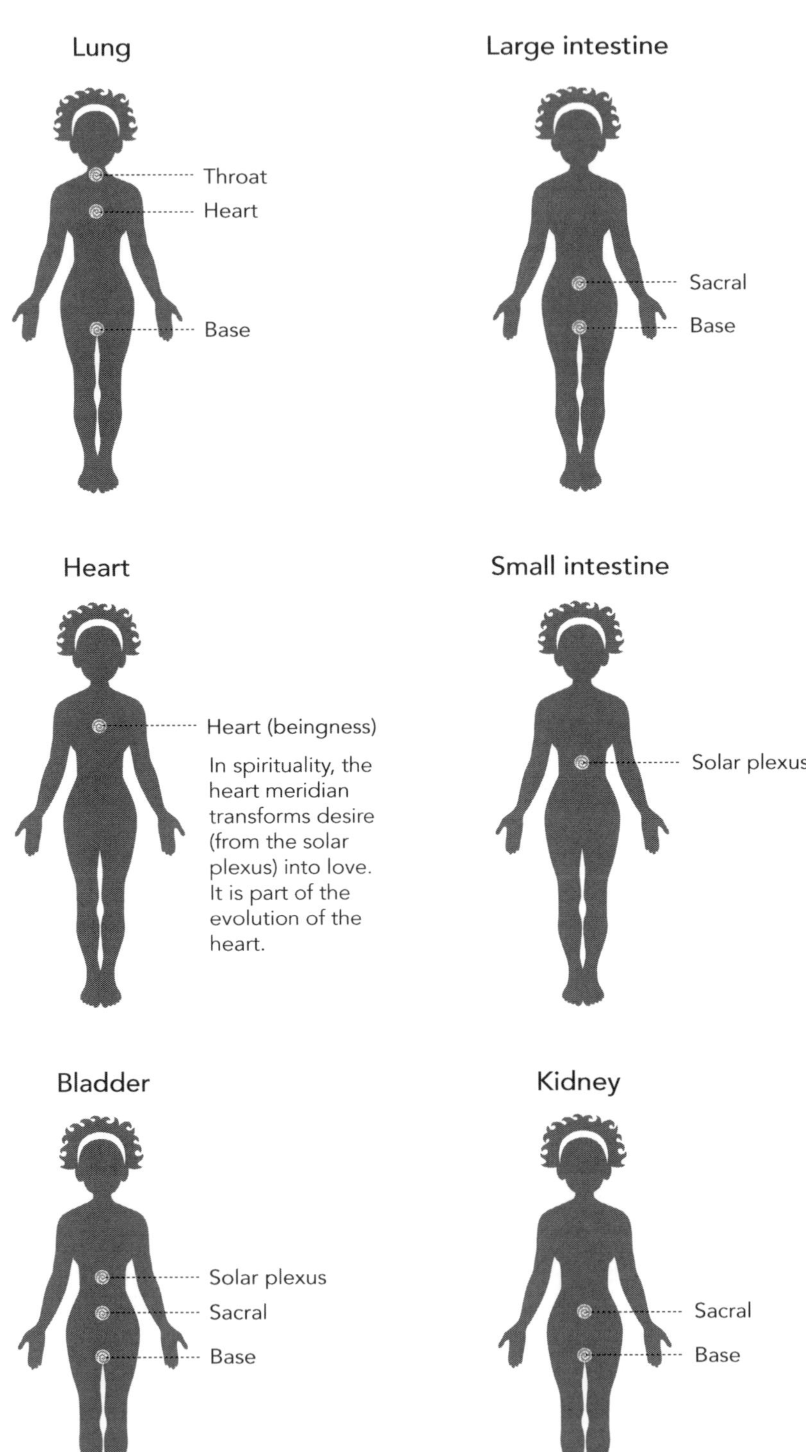

Figure 5: Meridians and their corresponding chakras

Stomach

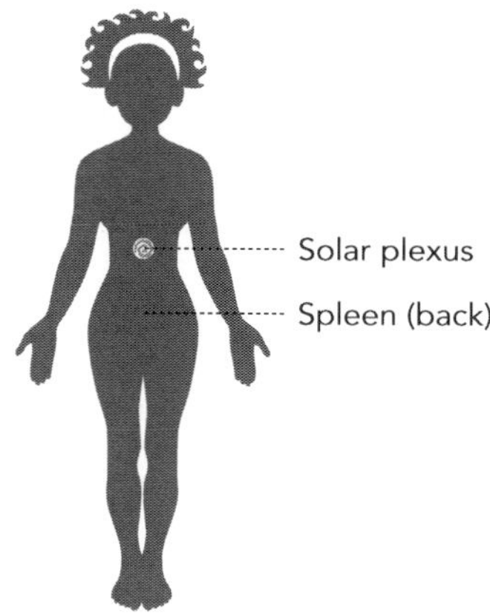

Spleen

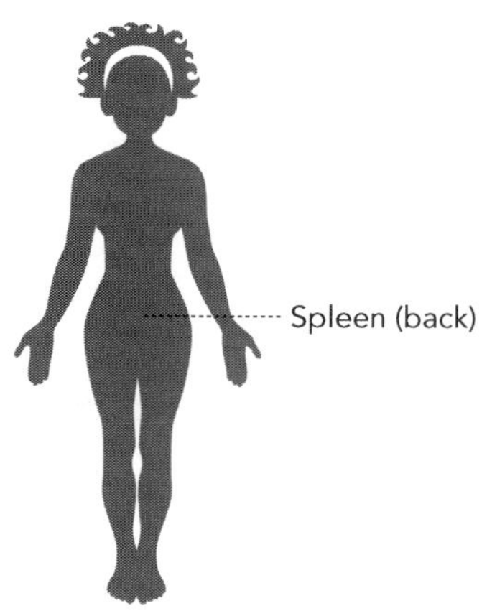

Pericardium

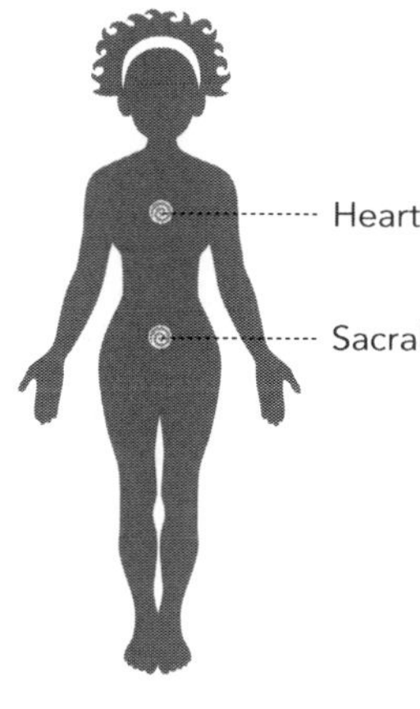

Triple heater

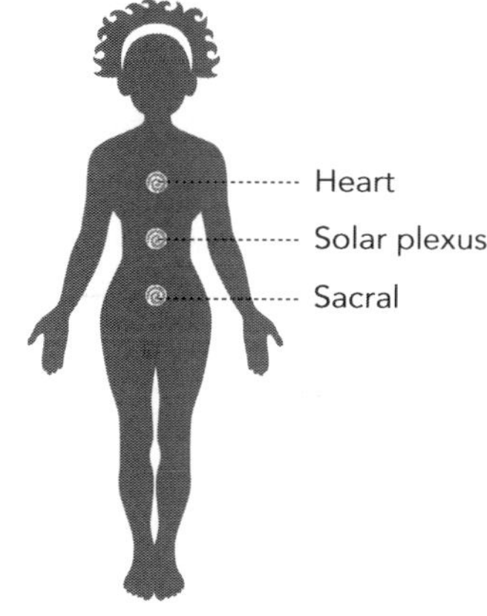

Gall bladder

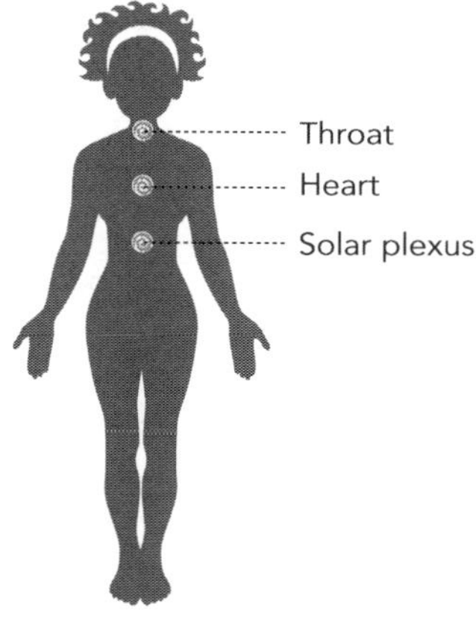

Liver

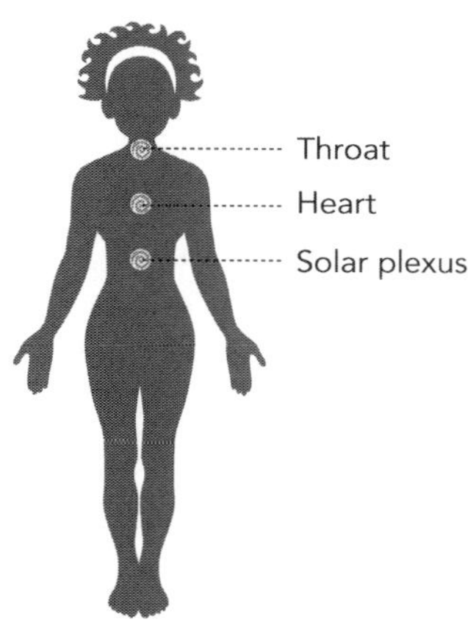

In energetic healing, we use the aura to assess where there is a lack of life-energy. Bella's vital life-energy was drained, and her body was struggling to support her. Her thoughts were somewhere else as she was constantly caught up in her anxieties, which also sapped her energy. She even spoke in slow monotones. In a way she had given up on life and felt overwhelmed with exhaustion. By listening and sensing Bella's emotive story, I was directed to the areas of her body where she was *feeling* the lack of energy and imbalance, and was correlating my knowledge of her meridians to the psychological challenges that were contributing to her unbalanced state.

Let's see just how much our bodies can reveal. While I looked at Bella's meridians I could see there was a lot going on. Her spleen told me there was *worry and anxiety, combined with over-thinking, which drained the body's vital energy and immune system.* Then when I looked at her stomach area I could sense *disappointment, an inability to digest emotions, resulting in poor digestion and bloating.* At the liver meridian that connects at the big toe there was *anger, inability to express self, shyness and mood swings.* Her lungs revealed *sadness, grief, and unfairness.* The large and small intestine indicated *poor self-worth/self-esteem, guilt processing and elimination of toxins, ingested emotionally, mentally and physically.*

Chakras

The above meridians had a connection physically and emotionally to Bella's solar plexus, heart, sacral and throat chakras. The energy of her lung meridian connected with her heart and throat chakras. Bella's issues made her feel ungrounded, which in turn was affecting her base-chakra energy, her whole foundation in life. She had temporarily lost her connection with the Earth, so she didn't have the security of her feet being planted firmly on the ground. This was a reason for her dull, pale and lacklustre appearance. Bella had lost heart, giving up on herself. It turned out that Bella had been going through a really difficult and drawn-out divorce, and she felt cheated and angry by her partner's manipulation, indiscretions and lies. She had lost faith in honest relationships.

Auras

Emotionally, Bella's energy was stuck in the astral body, the emotional layer of your aura. She was overloaded and overwhelmed with negative fears. Her constant self-limiting thoughts and beliefs (mental body) were draining her self-esteem and confidence, making it impossible for her to feel vibrant because the whole flow of her life-energy was blocked. It was as though Bella was punishing herself for not being good enough.

As Bella began to see how the different parts of her physical body were feeling, we were able to work with some positive insights to ground and balance her energy. By raising the life-energy in and around Bella's body and aura we were able to get her life-energy flowing again. She left feeling positive and empowered. Bella was amazed at just how much her body revealed, and how many keys it gave to her present problems.

33
Patterns of pain

The more we learn about the intricacies of our bodies, the more insight we have into what makes us tick, how sometimes we trip ourselves up, and where old patterns get lodged in our systems. There's no end to the information our body can reveal about us. You don't have to read auras to get a sense of what's happening, just listen closely to what your body is trying to tell you.

When a person talks to me about what's going on in their life, I listen for patterns. In other words, I listen for things that keep happening to the person and to others in their family. Family patterns are particularly significant, because whole areas of our lives are often influenced by our parents and family, even if they are not actively present in our lives. For example, there may be several generations of women who have suffered abusive relationships, or men who have endured partnerships where there has been little love or nurture.

Your aura hints at where your problem patterns lie.

When I looked at Keith's aura I could see he had difficulty stepping forward on his right foot, which is his male side. This told me there may be issues on his father's side of the family. Perhaps there was something going on with his father that needed to be addressed. Or perhaps there have been a number of men in the family over the generations who have been grappling with the same issues. It could also mean that he felt his masculinity was under attack by someone who was assertive or powerful, possibly a partner or his mother.

Becoming aware of that influence is your first step towards healing the issue. When you are not conscious of what is going on in your life, old patterns keep being repeated, and layer upon layer of pain build up. The result is a sense of confusion and chaos. Clients often tell me they feel they are hitting their head against a brick wall. They feel that the same thing happens over and over again to them, but feel powerless to change it. Becoming conscious of your unhelpful patterns is the key to dealing with them. You need to be more aware of how you feel and react in certain circumstances. When you bring a pattern to your attention, it is no longer hidden. It loses its power over you. As a result, you start to feel lighter and more free.

As an adult, you unconsciously parent from the pain of your childhood experiences.

Once Keith realised his life was limited because he couldn't be assertive, he started to notice each time he held back. As he became aware of his fears, he began to challenge the beliefs behind those unhelpful feelings. Keith started to question his family's pattern of not speaking out no matter how bad things got. By changing his thinking, he in turn felt more empowered and more inclined to speak up for himself. This rewiring created a shift in his energy, which gave him a sense of freedom and lightness and the confidence to explore the world in a new way. He felt he gained some control in his life.

In Laura's case the energy around her looked like it was compressed into a cylinder, pushed in on both the right and left sides of her aura. That told me something about the pressure she might be feeling from her mother and father. As we worked together Laura eventually saw that she was carrying a lot of grief and anger from old family issues that had never been dealt with. The backpack that I saw streaming with toxic water was literally behind her. When looking at the backpack, I felt as if she didn't want to see what she was carrying.

Often these painful patterns can seem so hard to address that it seems easier to ignore them. When you do this, however, your life-energy goes into keeping these hurts suppressed instead of helping you to lead a rich and fulfilling life. In Laura's case the pattern of holding her emotions deep inside, no matter what, had been handed down from parent to child, so nothing was ever resolved. Tragically, Laura's parents were proud of the fact that they'd never had a cross word. Even when Laura's brother distanced himself from the family and moved to the other side of the world, his parents said nothing.

Unless toxic patterns in families are dealt with, they will repeat themselves over and over again. You're probably aware of recurrent issues in your own family—and at work, which is another kind of family. These may be issues around powerlessness, deception, not feeling safe, bullying—the list goes on. One of the main reasons these patterns don't get dealt with is because they can be difficult to spot. You may be so used to them that you don't notice what's going on. Often your patterns go unnoticed until something big happens: you have a major shock; someone gets sick; you face separation or some other kind of relationship breakdown; or you're left to deal with a build-up of difficulties. Suddenly you're forced to question your life and decisions. This is exactly what happened to me.

Whatever your life experiences, they are stored in your cells as memory. As a practitioner I see constantly how this memory can be passed on from generation to generation because this cellular memory is stored in the DNA, so you can literally be living out the patterns of your ancestors. My job is to assist my clients to recognise these patterns, so they can be released. I might find, for example, that a client is blocked by traumatic experiences at three years of age, at five, and at nine. Once I'm aware of these patterns emerging at particular ages, I invite my client to think about their lives at three, five and nine, to see if these were significant times for them. This is important work and well worth the effort, because whenever we feel stressed or unhappy, we go back to these patterns. It's a kind of knee-jerk response. We keep on reacting the same way we did as a small child, when we first felt unloved, shamed, confused and so on.

When working with Keith it was clear to me that something distressing had happened to him when he was three. When we explored this time, we found that Keith had seen his father attacked violently when trying to break up a fight. Unfortunately Keith's father was badly injured, and during his recovery he kept saying that that was what a man gets when he takes action. Even though the event was long forgotten, whenever Keith was in a tricky situation, the only way he felt safe was to keep quiet.

We each have parts of us stuck in the past—our own past or that of our family. When I was working on myself, I discovered I was stuck at four years of age. At that time my mother wanted to get out of her marriage. One Saturday morning my dad had his suitcase in his hand and was finally leaving. Heartbroken at the prospect, I clung to him, screaming for him to stay. As it turned out Dad did turn around and come back.

However, as a four-year-old I felt powerless in this conflict. My sense of safety and security had been threatened. At the same time, my mother felt angry and disempowered when my father walked back through those front gates and into her life. The memory of that event was held in my cells in my throat, heart, stomach, reproductive organs and at the base of my spine. Later in life, I had health problems with these areas of my body. This is what is known as your body's biography of disease. *Each part of you that is sick holds a difficult part of your life story.*

My mother's story is important here. Born out of wedlock, and rejected by her biological father, the only acknowledgement she had from him was the monthly child-support payments sent to her grandmother, who brought her up. This continued until my mother was fifteen. She finally met her father briefly. It was the only time she ever saw him. After this meeting the financial support was withdrawn. Not surprisingly my poor mother felt completely disempowered by men. At that one and only meeting with her father, he told her he would deny any knowledge of her existence, and there would be no inheritance for her. That Saturday morning when Mum told my father to leave, though she may not have been consciously aware of it, she was trying to reclaim her power. In rejecting him, she was echoing and reflecting the deep pain she must have felt with her own father when he rejected her.

Even though Dad stayed, Mum did not feel secure or happy within herself, because on some level she was still the little girl who had been abandoned by a man. From an energy perspective, she suffered strong base-chakra traumas. That's because the base energy at the bottom of your spine relates to your family of origin and your sense of safety and security within that family. This energy centre is also connected to your sense of having the right to exist in the world. A violation of early stability, trust and hope in the future can set the foundations for major illness later on.

There were also problems with money, emotional wellbeing, and sense of self for Mum. These issues are related to the sacral and solar plexus chakras. The sacral chakra connects us to our sense of personal power. It's related to money, and to being supported in your relationships with others and ourselves. The solar plexus chakra is where we see all those issues related to our identity: our self-worth, self-esteem and self-confidence.

Unconsciously, my mum continued to play out her patterns of pain, and I inherited those patterns. What is also interesting is that my mother died of pancreatic cancer, a cancer that is hard to detect because it is hidden. In fact, one of the hallmarks of this cancer is that it often goes undetected. Her emotions were also hidden and her pain was buried deep in her stomach area that connects to the solar plexus chakra. On a physical level the solar plexus is related to our nervous system. There were many issues in Mum's life that she could not digest, so the sweetness and joy of life were hidden away.

Dad came back and stayed because of me. On the surface this might seem like a good thing, but from the tender age of four

I was told that I was responsible for my parents' relationship. A tall order! From that moment I took on the *belief that to be lovable I had to be overly responsible for other people*. My sacral and base chakras were *wounded* in this process because I believed that it was my responsibility to hold my family together, to keep everyone happy under the one roof.

Our emotional traumas start as seeds hidden in the mud of our deep-seated pain, and can take a whole lifetime of growth before they see the light of day. At whatever age we become stuck, it is most likely we will continue to respond as that part of us did at the age we were wounded. *Every time those around me were unhappy, my four-year-old self would come to the fore, and I would feel responsible for whatever was going on.* I would bend over backwards to make them feel better.

In her distress and pain, Mum would sometimes lash out. She could be controlling and dominating, and often I felt crushed. I understand now what she was going through, but as a child you don't see the bigger picture. From an early age I didn't feel safe around love, especially when care and affection were offered by women I considered powerful. I would become guarded, defensive, build walls around myself to keep myself safe. On the surface this seemed like a good way to go, but these walls became impenetrable. The beautiful dance in life of receiving as well as giving love and my ability to feel good about myself were all out of balance. I was living behind a smiling mask.

Thirty-four years later, I became so ill I nearly died—it was time to take a new path. I wanted to change the way my life was going. I learned to recognise old patterns and start the processes of forgiving and healing myself and those who had caused me pain. In these processes I took a giant leap forward and found that I now had more freedom than I ever felt possible.

I realised I could create new patterns and make more positive, informed choices in my life. This shift allowed me to be much more loving and compassionate towards myself.

If only we realised how often we keep playing out our childhood wounds—physically, emotionally and mentally—things would be so much easier. Even though the intense feelings and the energy around each trauma are locked away deep inside us, we continue to play out the same old patterns sparked by those traumas in our relationships. When we have difficulties with a relationship, or when we feel tired, drained, anxious or depressed, it may be a sign that we are not coping with our repetitive patterns.

Petra came to see me when her long-term relationship ended. This break-up was the third in ten years, and while Petra was the one who had left, she feared that she had no hope of finding a partner she could settle with. In the clairvoyant state before she arrived, I'd seen a severe constriction of energy down the right side of her body, as well as what looked like an arrow in her right shoulder. I sensed difficulty with a powerful man who had caused her great pain.

Sure enough, as Petra talked about her early life, she said her father had died suddenly when she was two, leaving her mother totally distraught. Petra's mother began to bring various men home, but the relationships never lasted more than a couple of months. Just as Petra started to feel comfortable with the new man, her mother would ask him to leave. Within weeks there would be another man on the scene. Petra learned early that it was unsafe to care for a man for more than a short time, because he was bound to leave.

Of course, this was an old pattern that was no longer useful to Petra. Her problem was that part of her was stuck at the age of three or four, as that was the only way she knew how to behave. Once this was brought to light, Petra could see the pattern she had been playing out all these years. With this reconnection to her past pattern of pain she was able to release the past trauma, and change to a healthier way of relating to the men in her life. As it turned out, Petra reunited with the man she'd recently asked to leave, they made their peace and began to move forward together.

Time and again I see this kind of thing happening for my clients. Once they recognise their patterns and realise they no longer need them, they release that entire past trauma, so that their lives can be full of joy instead of pain. It can be tricky to identify what those patterns are, and you may need some help to uncover them, but it's one of the most valuable exercises you'll ever do. It will change your life in ways you have only dreamed of before.

34

Stairway to the stars

Everything we have examined so far is linked to your soul. When I talk of soul I mean your spiritual essence, what makes you human. It is the life-energy that permeates your whole body, sustaining you. Ancient wisdom teachings describe the soul as neither spirit nor matter, but rather as the relationship between both. It is that part that propels you forward, the sudden knowing when you don't know what to do. It contains all the impressions, influences and experiences you have while on Earth. After your death, your qualities, knowledge and characteristics are re-absorbed into your spirit. All energy returns to its source.

The time spent in the spirit world, or heaven, is called *involution.* This is when you don't have a physical body. When you reincarnate at the time of your birth, you once again tread the path of *evolution* on planet Earth. This allows you to continue your soul's development as a human being. Your soul is important in everyday life. Though you might not be aware of it, we often speak of the soul. When someone or something touches us, we describe it as reaching the depths of our soul. Or when a person is talking, we may feel as though he or she were speaking to our soul. A newborn baby may be described as having the face of an old soul. Your soul is the most profound and enduring part of you, it's your X-factor. By contrast when a person is out of synch they may say, 'There's a part of me missing', or 'No matter what I do there is no sense of satisfaction'. Or you may worry about going down a certain path lest you lose your soul. While soul is not tangible—it's wordless and formless—it is an inner knowing.

Now we get to the really exciting bit. How can we bring everything we have learned together in a powerful way that will serve ourselves and others? To do this you need to bring the physical you (personality) and the spiritual aspects of yourself together. Ancient wisdom calls this stairway the 'rainbow bridge'. Let's look at how to build this stairway.

You are already connected to your soul through the circuits between your aura, your chakras and the many meridians throughout your body. These subtle electrical pathways are called *nadis*. We have 72,000 of them in all. These delicate pathways enable your physical and subtle bodies to communicate. You can't see them, but they are there.

Your soul is fuelled by the highest form of energy in the universe. It's a bit like putting the best fuel available in your car. When you have an inspired idea or goal that is *genuinely* soulful, you activate threads of light. These intricate threads link these aspirations to your soul. Over time, and with patience and effort, the threads of light within us grow into a luminous beacon of light, just like a lighthouse in the darkness. This beautiful expanded light then helps align your soul with your personality. Your heart is the gateway for this process. When you follow your heart, the light grows within you. When the light begins to expand in your heart, it illuminates your physical and spiritual selves, bringing them powerfully together.

Your inspired thoughts and aspirations become a magnetic force continually attracting more light and more good towards you. This is the secret of the ancient law of attraction. As you simply become more *aware* or *open* to the magical possibilities in life, the more you can create wonderful possibilities that you hardly dared to dream of. There are many ways you can connect with your soul's energy: through meditation, personal growth, prayers, invocations, service to humanity, animals or the environment, forgiveness, gratitude and right human relationships. You practise right human relations every time you take responsibility for your actions and when you strive to develop honesty and integrity in all your dealings with yourself and others.

How can we make all this happen? As we've already noted, to feel truly in balance and empowered your personality needs to align with your soul. An easy way to visualise this process is to imagine two triangles. This first triangle represents your personality or lower self. The three points of this lower triangle are related to your physical self, your body, your instincts, your mind and emotions. The base of the triangle represents your *physical body* (base chakra). Your physical body is your foundation as it's the vehicle you use to get around in your daily life. It's a home and transport for your soul/spirit.

The right-hand side of the triangle represents your *emotional/ desire body*, which stores all your emotions, past and present, including how you feel about life. As it deals with emotions it is connected to the sacral chakra.

Figure 6: The vital link

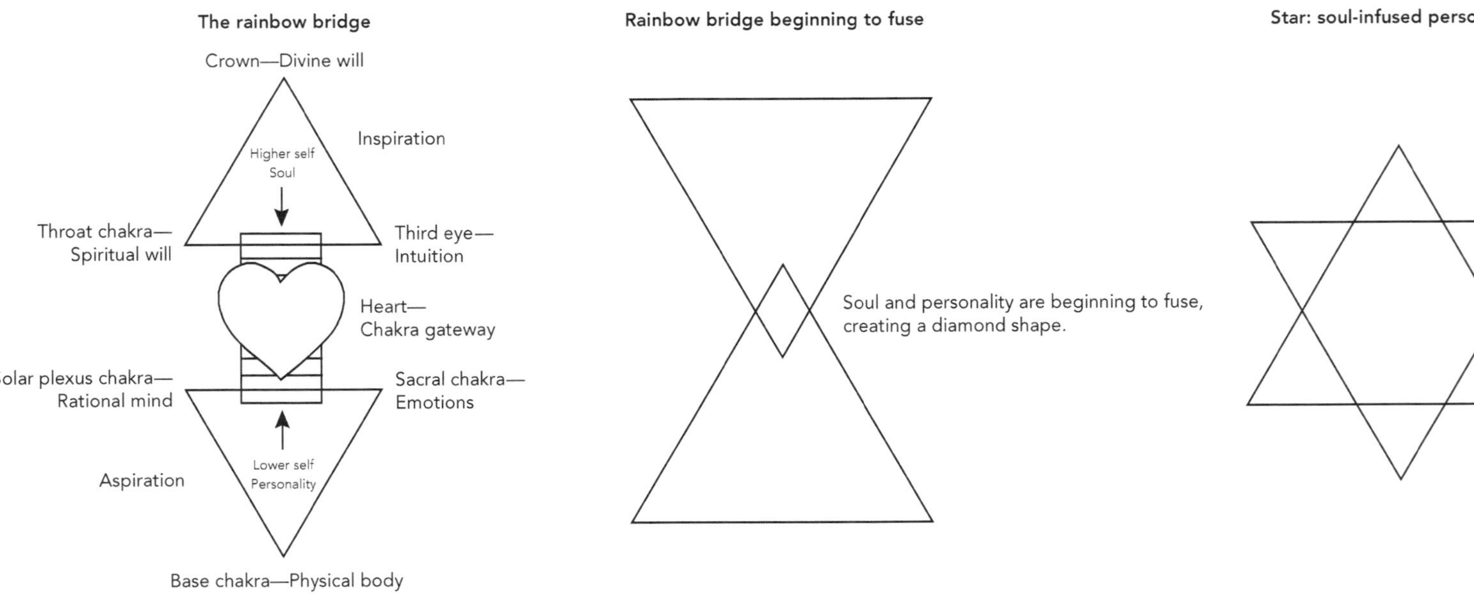

A person who hasn't consciously commenced the soul's journey/purpose

Positive and constructive work is being done. Person focused on 'right human relationships'.

A star of light emerges

The left-hand side of this triangle relates to your *mental body* and is the storehouse of your thoughts. Because it governs the way you think, it is connected to the solar plexus. It holds all your past and present attitudes and beliefs and influences your thought processes. *We all think and analyse differently simply because we are wired differently.*

These three aspects of the triangle make up our personality (lower self).

As I've already mentioned, the *heart* is the *gateway* via your feeling nature to your *higher self/soul.*

Your soul is housed in your spiritual bodies. These spiritual bodies relate to the upper triangle, which like a flash of divine inspiration points down to Earth like an arrow. When talking about the three aspects contained within this spiritual triangle, we look at your *soul's* energy, past and present.

These three wonderful aspects or bodies are connected to your spiritual resources, treasures, talents, gifts and creativity. They make up your *true* identity and *your divinity.* Let's see what each of these spiritual bodies relates to.

Your higher self is the container of your hidden wisdom. Your higher self contains the blueprint of your life's journey—only via your personality can you access the soul.

At the top of the triangle is the *mind of God,* the oneness of all life, also known as divine will, which is connected to the crown chakra. *Spiritual love* on the right side of the triangle is connected to the kind of love-wisdom we associate with Christ and Buddha. When this high quality of love is evoked, passion becomes compassion and conditional love is transformed into unconditional love. It is all encompassing. This beautiful, all-embracing love is connected to the third-eye chakra which brings clear insight and the ability to recognise truth. *Spiritual will* on the left-hand side of the triangle is the power to do good for goodness' sake. It is an area that relates to divine will as opposed to will based on ego.

Your spiritual will is connected to the throat chakra, and refers to your communication on all levels.

Your spiritual bodies are the storehouse of your soul's energy, past and present.

True intuition comes directly from the soul and allows you to see and know your inner truth, seeing life as energy. Clear seeing also comes from the soul. It allows you to let go of judgment and to operate with loving detachment towards yourself and others, instead of being needy and critical. This is possible when you allow these three very special qualities to inform your work, your relationships, your passions.

Ultimately, the point of your life's journey is to bring *soul* and *personality* together. When these two triangles begin to merge, the point where they overlap looks like a diamond. At this stage of your journey you have made contact with your soul's energy and are steadily in the process of building your rainbow bridge between your higher self and lower self. The two triangles create a six-pointed *star of light* at your heart centre creating a soul-infused personality. When this happens the heart's code or mantra becomes '*I am love*'. The light generated by this alignment of your personality and soul draws the soul into the centre of who you are—into the middle of the diamond star. That's why we are all stars in the making!

When your personality is infused with the light of your soul, you use your personality in a positive way, radiating light, love, harmony and inspiration to others. You touch people's hearts and without even realising it, you feed people's spirits. We all know people like this. Soul-infused personalities have a strong sense of their life purpose. There's a healing quality about them.

The fusion of your soul and personality is an ongoing process, which continues to deepen as you progress. By taking time out to be quiet, to mediate, to work on yourself, to give back, you create more light in your physical body, literally transforming your physical atoms into spiritual atoms, until you become enlightened. The further you progress the more life flows. Your struggles lessen, synchronicity becomes commonplace, your life direction is clearer.

The development of your star of light takes place over lifetimes, for most of us at least.

As your awareness changes you experience real *freedom*. The load you've been carrying feels lighter, now those past concerns are behind you. As you continue to forge new frontiers, exciting opportunities become available to you because your soul is able to draw these to you. It's as if you've been asleep, and suddenly you wake up, and a more joyous life begins to unfold.

35

Your very own yellow brick road

Emma was attending a class where she was learning to connect with her inner guidance. She asked if her guides could prove they were real by playing one of her favourite songs on the radio while she was driving home after class. To her surprise, not one but four songs that had special meaning for her were played during the journey. Each song was a song of the heart. Emma couldn't believe these synchronicities, especially as she had been having difficulty opening her heart and trusting others. But the magic didn't stop there. While she was driving to work the next day she stopped at traffic lights and as she gazed out of the car window she noticed a tree with outstretched branches. Through the gap in the branches the sun's rays were flooding the ground below, creating a beautiful heart shape. Emma knew this was a truly inspired moment—she'd driven past this same tree every day and had never seen anything like it!

When you make that first connection to your higher self it can feel like a light going on or a door opening. Some people experience it as an explosion of white and golden light. For me it was like a cascade of liquid gold, pouring down through the top of my head. My body began to rock gently and I just knew something very beautiful had just happened. It was profound and uplifting. For some this is a euphoric experience. Others react with a tsunami of tears. However you experience this beautiful connection you know something out of the ordinary has just happened.

Light-filled soulful experiences can also happen when there is no logical or rational explanation. You know when you're having one of those moments because time appears to stand still, or your perceptions expand a little or a lot. This is the perfect space for synchronicities to happen. When you begin to experience synchronistic events that have an unmistakable impact, and you begin to welcome them into your life so that they become the norm, you have moved to the next stage of soul growth—that of trusting your inner wisdom and guidance. You are tuning into the wonderful flow of life-energy on offer. It's such a feel-good moment when you begin to *trust* the intelligence and wisdom of the world you live in to support you.

Integrate your synchronicities

So, what's the purpose of synchronicity? It's like hidden keys. Synchronicity comes into your life, not just to delight you, but to help you learn and grow. You do this by observing or noticing your feelings and awareness to synchronistic events. The more mindful you are about how you respond to these simple but powerful occurrences the more wisdom and insight you'll get out of them. Use your intuitive power to listen carefully to what is being said around you. Take in what is relevant and meaningful to your current situation or your soulful questions.

Be open and curious to the way the universe speaks to you. Signs can appear as repetitive number sequences, words or catchy phrases or they may be a melody that just drops into your head. Start a daily soul diary so that you can reflect back on the many tiny miracles you've experienced and what each one taught you.

Along the way try always to remain open to new attitudes and beliefs, as this will keep the positive life-energy moving and flowing. Imbue everything you do with soulfulness and you'll find that it will bring a new beauty and power to all you do. When you are careful to follow your soul's promptings, it will speed up your personal development and fusion between your personality and soul. All kinds of unexpected opportunities, sudden bursts of inspiration and acts of kindness will come your way.

This is what Calvin, one of my students, discovered. Calvin had been enrolled in a psychic development course at another college, and had been experiencing repetitive dreams where he kept hearing the name Annie. He didn't know any Annies at that point and there were none listed at the college. Just before the new semester began Calvin got another message to enrol at the college where an Annie was lecturing. He had been reluctant to trust the messages he was receiving from his intuitive prompting and guides, but this time he did, and that is how he came to be in my class.

In one class, I was telling a story about the death of my daughter's friend due to a motorbike accident. For most of the course, Calvin had not said a word, but during this story he became very animated, hanging off my every word. It turned out that he'd had a similar accident to my daughter's friend, and he lived on the same street and was the same age as my daughter's friend, and also rode a motorbike. The synchronicity of the two events was a chilling awakening, which also validated Calvin's ability to hear and trust the messages he had been getting from his guides.

It's important to trust your inner promptings as they are the signposts to your soul. Often at the time the small pieces of a puzzle don't make sense. It may take a little while for the big picture to emerge. It may even be years down the track. But it's worth the wait as the outcome is always so much better. Patience and trust are the keys. My class story allowed Calvin to trust his intuition and guidance.

Another such moment occurred when a lady from the Charismatic Society placed one of her hands gently on my shoulder. Suddenly, my life-energy felt like it was drawn out of my body into a ball of brilliant white light. In that moment I felt fully at one with the whole of life. Time stood still. There was an awareness of me, but I had no feelings of the physical restriction or the pain that I had been experiencing in my back, stomach and arm. It melted away. My physical body expanded. It felt boundaryless. I experienced a real sense of freedom as I drew closer to the centre of this white light, which appeared to be suspended less than a metre from my physical body. In this soulful moment my body was still sitting on the couch and the lady's hand was still on my left shoulder. The peace, love and nurturing I felt left me buzzing for four to five hours. It was truly blissful.

These extraordinary soul experiences often coincide with an overwhelming recognition that *you are loved*, but have failed to understand it. You are then able to allow this love to warm your space, to feel more hopeful, more inspired, kinder in the future. Basically, the journey of the soul is coming home to love. Seeing the real beauty and wonder in life and experiencing love are in fact the same thing. *Consciousness* and *love* are one and the same.

36

Clearing out the cobwebs

We've covered a great deal of ground. How then do we put it all together? It's a bit like night time when you walk into a dark empty room in your house and you flick on the electricity switch. Light floods into the room and suddenly you can see. If you have a high-voltage light bulb, your room will be well lit. If you have a low-voltage light bulb, the lesser light will create shadows or darkness in the room.

When you travel the spiritual path, the emerging light of your soul highlights your positive qualities. It also brings to your attention the shadowy pockets where you have let the cobwebs grow. Let's call these cobwebs your unaddressed issues or patterns. When you address your patterns, you create an opening for the light of your soul to enter. You begin to see more clearly and everything feels brighter.

Your patterns of woundedness—the cobwebs—can happen at any age from birth onwards. Left unattended they become solid, crystallised, frozen forms of blocked life-energy that create dark shadowy patches in your aura. You feel tired, stressed, angry and/or unhappy. The interesting thing about your patterns is that they are really good at hiding away and coming out in your attitudes, behaviour and beliefs. When examined a little closer, these beliefs often form through anxiety, fear or a need to be in control.

Each moment of the day you are reading the energy patterns of yourself and others through your solar plexus chakra, which is connected to your nervous system and your emotional self. Every time you experience a situation similar to your first wounding, you unconsciously react in the same way you did back then. You become upset, angry, afraid and so on. When you can't diffuse these emotional and mental patterns, this negative energy lodges itself in your physical and subtle bodies. Over time the areas where these patterns lodge themselves may become sensitive spots in or on your physical body, even to touch.

In essence, we make these sensitive spots—shame, guilt, trust, betrayal, anger, resentment, jealousy and failure—our no-go zones. *They are the buried or cut-off energetic parts of your self.* Whenever you are reluctant to revisit trapped feelings associated with your hidden pain, this is a sign that it's exactly what you need to address. It takes courage to do this because, invariably, pain has tremendous *fear* attached to it. And if it's not addressed, it will make life painful on every level. In some cases, the fear your patterns generate can surround your entire aura like a black cloud. To shift your energy you need to feel the fear and confront it anyway, or at least try to establish its root cause, so that you can transform it, see it in a different light. At the end of the day, *fear is a word that gives you freedom to express areas of your life that require review.* The crazy thing is that often when you do touch the no-go areas, the pain is nowhere near as hard to take as you imagine it to be: instead of falling to pieces, you'll feel it's a huge relief.

If you're feeling continually frustrated, lack motivation, are failing to thrive, suffer from addictions, laziness, depression or apathy, you may be suppressing your life-energy. You could also be stuck if you often experience a sense of silent seething, personal frustration or lack of being able to make things happen. It's important to remember that what you don't own about yourself, you have to deal with in those around you! Martin Lass, a soul-centred astrologer, tells us: 'When we are unable to deal with our wounds and blockages, we find ourselves blaming everything and everybody outside ourselves for the way we are and the way our lives are.'

So, when a personal growth challenge appears in your life, don't despair. There may be several gifts on offer. When you muster up the courage to face your issues, you will open the door to new soul gifts and qualities that you never knew you had.

Connecting the dots from a past trauma to a present experience can be empowering. One powerful way of doing this is by developing the art of listening when you are with others. Why? Because the advice you give can be exactly what you need to hear yourself! Try it next time you are generously handing out that well-intentioned speech. You may be surprised at what is revealed. You will also find the universe brings you the exact person, at the right time, for the exact situation that needs to be resolved.

If you seriously want to make progress you also need to take charge of your life. When you fail to take responsibility for past hurts, you give your personal power away. Even though you may have been badly hurt by others, you have the choice here and now to do something about it, or remain the victim. Where you don't take up your personal power, you'll find there are plenty of others that will do it for you. Perhaps now is a good time to see where you need to be more assertive in your life. As the penny drops, the victim can retire.

One of the struggles you may feel is the tension between what your personality wants (past crystallised patterns) as opposed to that of your soul. The personality has a vested interest in perpetuating old habits, so it can *control* you. You see, the personality doesn't like change. Your soul, by contrast, simply wants to set you free. Why not embrace the change!

Often you don't know your own inner strength until its tested!

To allow soul into your life you need to pay attention to what you're doing so you become aware of your patterns. This takes effort and honesty. This also means taking responsibility for yourself, and being compassionate and patient. This isn't about getting rid of your personality but simply tempering it with the wisdom and insight of your soul. The wiser you are, the easier it is to leave behind your excess baggage and travel light.

Understanding my past patterns opened the door to my future and the work I do now. There is always light at the end of the tunnel even if you can't see it at the time! Letting go, forgiveness, change and surrender kept my dream alive. Courage, discipline and focus made the rewards well worth the journey. The path to self-love, self-healing and self-understanding can lead you out of the maze of poor outcomes to inner peace and inspired living.

37

The magic of mud maps

You cannot teach man anything, you can only help him discover it within himself.

—Galileo

Let me tell you a little about the mud maps I do for my clients. I call them mud maps because like the lotus flower we have the capacity to rise out of the depths of the mud we find ourselves in, and emerge as a rare and beautiful flower. Out of the darkness the lotus reaches up and opens in the light, and so too can you in all sorts of wonderful ways.

When I draw mud maps for clients prior to their session, I connect to their *cellular memories* or *core patterns*, which are driven by outmoded *beliefs*. Each cellular memory has a time frame attached to it, pinpointing specific events that have occurred in the past and that are still impacting on the client's current situation and emotions. The repetitive themes and stories that I pick up on when I do a reading may relate to work,

Figure 7: Fran's mud map

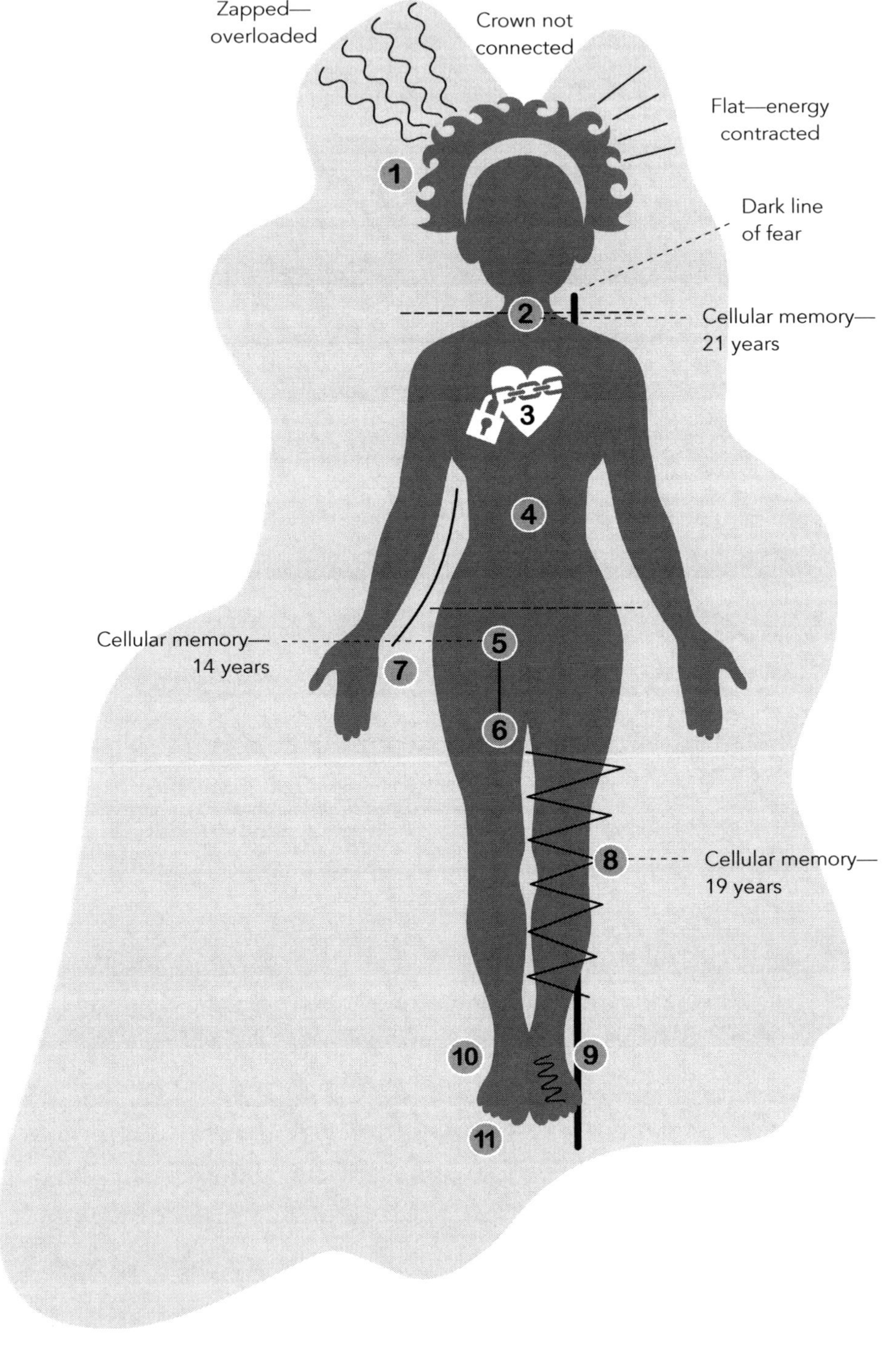

1. Third-eye chakra—not open/off centre

Fran's past life is contributing to her present frustration and clarity. She is saying that she trusts her intuition, but it is not an integrated trust. I sense self-doubt.

2. Throat chakra—energy cut at the throat
Cell memory: 21 years

This chakra is open at the back, but only open slightly at the front. It is like an old gramophone; in place but not fully working. There is a dark line of fear running down the left side of the body. I sense a shock connected to both the spiritual realm and guidance.

3. Heart chakra

I sense a locked chain around Fran's heart: a 'holding heart' that retains unconscious memories of past lives in order that she isn't hurt in this life. Past lives act as a mirror to a person's present situation.

4. Solar plexus chakra

Fran's guidance acknowledges the work she has done on her solar plexus area, which is good. She needs to work on bringing energy from this area up to the heart. I sense the words 'compromising love' and the question 'Who are you compromising?'

5–6. Sacral and base chakras
Cell memory: 14 years

These appear pushed out of alignment from the central channel. Both chakras' energy have disconnected from Fran's upper torso, creating a misalignment and making it difficult for Fran to ground. She is dealing with control issues in relationships.

7. Pain in right shoulder

I see pain running down from Fran's shoulder to her little finger.

8. Left leg

Fran's left leg feels fractured, her energy squeezed like an accordion. She is really struggling with her feminine self, and needs to let go and surrender! I sense indecision connected to this leg to do with Fran's spirituality—the energy has been cut off. The left knee holds a cell memory of 19 years.

9. Left foot

I sense that Fran is not accepting or receiving love. The foot appears 'mushy', soaking in swampy green water, like she is wearing a hospital slipper. This foot is floating in emotional toxicity. (These are Fran's thoughts I am receiving.)

10. Right foot—heel

Fran is literally 'digging in her heels', using the energy of her masculine side aggressively. The right heel appears symbolically bruised from this repeated action.

11. Right foot—toe

I feel anger in Fran's liver, and her spleen draining her energy. Her gall bladder meridian, connected to her bruised heel, reveals Fran's frustration at her inability to make decisions. I sense the words 'unjustness' and 'unfairness' associated with this toe. These emotions in turn affect the solar plexus, heart and throat chakras. There is personal anxiety and sadness around this toe.

relationships or family issues. These cellular memories have a habit of manifesting as pain in the body. During the session, we work on recognising those patterns so they can be healed.

My mud map is basically an *energetic scan* and *assessment of the client's aura*, not dissimilar to an X-ray. I start with a simple stick man representing the client's body, then I build up the information as I read their inner and outer energy fields, recording my sensory impressions that I see clairvoyantly. My initial impressions, written quickly as bullet points, are then expanded on; as I discuss the person's mud map in our session together, I add details to the initial stick figure, filling in details and drawing as I go. Each mud map is unique, because we are all unique and our energy is always in a state of flux and change. While cellular memories may at first reveal uncomfortable and painful patterns, working through them gives my client the opportunity to release their hidden potential.

The numbers circled in Figure 7 relate to the areas of my client's energy fields—I'll call her Fran—in which core patterns were revealed to me, and where the time frames relating to the cellular memories were discovered. Understanding when something first happened is a key component to the patterns revealed in a session.

There is also a cast of characters—departed parents, partners, ex-partners, work colleagues, children and others—who leave their mark energetically in a person's aura. They are often very vocal telepathically, wanting to make a contribution to the healing session. These spirit souls tend to become close to the person's aura as I am drawing. Generally their presence is an indication of the *love* shared between them. In our sessions, both parties—the living and the departed—contribute to the healing of several lifetimes of memories because, as we've seen, often these issues are part of the patterns that have developed over generations. Amazing really!

Let's have a look at Figure 7, in which Fran's most recent mud map is depicted (I'd previously drawn three mud maps for Fran, but, with all of us, there are always more layers to work on).

Fran initially made an appointment to see me because she was feeling blocked. I assessed her energy before she arrived, and this new mud map revealed that Fran was dealing with some deeper layers of the same old issues, which connected to her past in this life as well as to those of previous lives. What had occurred in the past was now affecting her present life. I studied her energetic patterns: though they had formed at different *points in time*, the issues were exactly the same.

As you can see in Figure 7, I noticed that her third-eye chakra was partially closed and off-centre, telling me that she was having difficulty trusting her intuition. This made her vulnerable and full of self-doubt. I saw Fran in a past life jailed, chained and held captive. This traumatic experience had impacted on her third-eye chakra. As I continued to scan her energy fields, more information filtered down about her third eye. It turned out that in a past life Fran had abused her sight, so there was a karmic debt to be paid. This was now creating feelings of frustration, trust, betrayal and regret.

Her throat chakra was only partially open, meaning that Fran was experiencing a communication blockage of some sort. I could see that this had its origins in an experience that occurred in Fran's life 21 years earlier. I could also see that Fran's heart was 'locked', retaining past memories so that she was unable to resolve current issues. Fran's solar-plexus chakra showed that she had made some progress in that area, which was good, but she needed to work on bringing energy from there to her heart. Both the sacral and base chakras were out of alignment, indicating that Fran finds it very difficult to 'ground' herself. I could see that she was having control issues in her relationships, stemming from an incident that had occurred 14 years ago. I could sense pain in her shoulder, running down to her little finger, and her left leg appeared fractured, the energy having been squeezed out of it. This told me that Fran needs to come to terms with her feminine side, an issue with which she was currently battling. This was confirmed by her right heel, which was symbolically bruised due to repeated blows ('digging her heels in') to this area, where Fran has been using her masculine energy aggressively. Fran's left foot appeared mushy, and encased in what looked to be a hospital slipper, floating in emotional toxicity. Her right toe revealed a residual anger in her liver and spleen, draining her of energy. There was also personal anxiety and sadness around this toe.

Fran's cellular memory also revealed major issues about *men and relationships*. A few beliefs that kept Fran's energy stuck included: 'All men that I'm close to leave me', 'Men aren't safe', 'Men reject me', 'Men abuse me', 'I have to fight to survive', 'I'm never good enough', 'I'm not worthy of love'. These had coloured all her relationships from her early childhood experiences right back to those of her past lives. Unconsciously Fran was creating the situations in her male relationships at work and in the family that reflected her patterns and beliefs.

As we unveiled these unhelpful cellular memories, we noted the emerging theme of a seven-year cyclical pattern with the men in her life. At seven, Fran's father left, they became estranged and had no further communication. At fourteen, her closest brother, whom she loved dearly, distanced himself from the family unit, leaving Fran shocked and deeply saddened. At twenty-one, she left her boyfriend and was retrenched from her job. Also at twenty-one, Fran had a traumatic accident when she fell off a horse, leaving her with injuries to her head, neck, right shoulder and all down the right side of her body. At twenty-eight, Fran married, then was retrenched again! (Echoes of not being good enough.) When she was thirty-five she sued her workplace for unfair dismissal.

Fran, while sobbing with relief, was shocked. She finally understood what had been happening for most of her life and spontaneously allowed the locked cellular memories to release. Fran could now see the relationship between her need to control out of fear and the damage it created for herself and the men around her.

Not surprisingly, Fran had become numb—physically mentally and emotionally—with the pain of her journey. Unplugged from her own life-energy and that of her soul it was difficult to trust that life would support her.

The male issues that Fran was dealing with were *reflected and carried* in her male (right-hand side) energy, restricting her forward direction. She spoke that she was tired of everything in her life being so hard. I'd picked this up in the energy around her right foot where she was digging her heels in and using her male energy aggressively, making her right heel feel sore and bruised. As it turned out, Fran was literally trying to put her foot down and control the timing of a new innovative project she was developing for children. She found herself constantly being blocked, although the project was to assist and serve humanity. Fran found out that universal timing was a whole different matter. She was struggling with her impatience and felt that this was the cause of her blocked male energy. By connecting back to her cellular memory we found the underlying key.

In summarising Fran's chart, the main points that arose were:

- Fran is asking a lot of questions but not accepting the answers that come to her.
- Fran's guidance is trying to support her, but she doesn't want to listen to the higher authority of divine timing. Patience is required at this time.
- Fran has become far more sensitive to her current local environment.
- Fran is dealing with issues from past lives, and her past in this life. She is walking in parallel states of consciousness.
- I saw Fran in a past life being held captive; chained and restricted.
- Her present issues are connected to her childhood and adolescence, and are affecting Fran's throat, sacral and base chakras.

Fran had some amazing insights along our mud-map journey. It demanded courage and strength to work with these uncomfortable patterns, but was worth it. In our last meeting Fran said she had come to a place of just being—and was loving it.

The night after her mud-map consultation, Fran asked for a message to help her release and clear this past life once and for all. Standing barefoot on the earth, thoughts of her dark past filled Fran's mind. She immediately felt the guilt and shame of her actions, and tears flowed. Using her breath to exhale the negativity she felt in her body, Fran began to feel lighter and freer. Her chronic lower back pain left her that night—and it hasn't troubled her since.

38

How we carry our patterns of pain

Once you become aware of your woundedness, you begin to see your patterns emerge. One of the most powerful is the *dance of the drama triangle,* which consists of a persecutor, victim and rescuer. Sometimes these patterns can continue generation after generation, sometimes lifetime after lifetime, masking your hidden potential. Childhood hurts that are not dealt with will impact on your adult life over and over. You get caught up in these patterns because they're stored in your cellular memory, influencing the way you think, react and feel. As you grow, these patterns define your perceptions of who you are. They feed into the limited thoughts you have about yourself, based on pain and suffering and define how you operate in life. The important thing to remember is that they're not *you.*

A great first step to take is to become more aware of people and situations that make you feel uncomfortable or out of control. Notice the area of your life where you feel most vulnerable when someone pushes your buttons. Then see if you can find a word that would best describe your feelings at that time. Try to become aware of the impact these feelings have on your everyday life, the way you react to your partner, boss, neighbours or kids. Notice the role you play with your partner. Are you constantly rescuing them or are you a victim of their indiscretions or abusive temper? Do you have a history of working with people who treat you with disrespect? If you're in a position of authority, are you always pushing the boundaries with disregard for others? This indicates you're playing persecutor right now. Or perhaps you're the rescuer who feels you have to make everything right for everyone else. Do you always feel helpless or powerless to make your own decisions? This means you've fallen into the role of victim.

One of my most painful life moments happened when I was four years old, when Dad threatened to leave home. This was when my *first* triangle dance was set up between Mum, Dad and myself. I became a *victim of circumstance* between my parents and their unaddressed issues. The role of the victim continued well into my late forties, causing me pain and suffering.

Your key contestants

The dance comes into play when there are three people projecting and mirroring the same pattern, such as low self-worth, the need to be in control, or being ruled by fear or anxiety. These patterns can be fuelled by family beliefs and attitudes. You may see being in love as becoming a doormat, or having to give up friends and interests, and so on. You'll know when you're in a triangle dance—it's an area in your life where you feel continually compromised, angry and resentful. And just like a revolving door, your life circumstances keep repeating themselves, because you don't feel empowered enough to step out.

I was seven when I first consciously witnessed the dance of the drama triangle being played out by my parents. At the time I had no idea about the complexities of the situation, but I felt the injustice, manipulation and deceit all the same. It registered in my body and aura, and took up residence there. George Gintilas, a body psychotherapist, tells us, 'our immediate family has a major influence in what develops and what doesn't develop in our emotional maturity.'

I stood in the doorway of my brother's room, listening to Mum describe the ways she deliberately manipulated Dad, using my brother like a pawn in a chess game. I couldn't believe what I was hearing. In that moment my seven-year-old self registered shock and fear. I had the sense of being overwhelmed by a situation that I was powerless to change. My immediate response in later life was always to withdraw at any sign of conflict. From this point on I became fearful and worried whenever my parents got angry and emotional. It was as though a part of me was still in shock, numbed and frozen. My ability to feel safe, let alone respond whenever I faced conflict, had been put on hold. Each volatile incident with my parents only added to my sense of fear. The stuck energy from my seven-year-old self registered as trauma in my body and auras. Later in my life it impeded the flow of life-energy through my body—causing a terminal illness.

When I was placed in similar situations as an adult, it was like someone was pushing my buttons. I reacted with fear and consequently withdrew. My seven-year-old self had learned to tread lightly before responding or taking action. I lost my childhood sense of fun and spontaneity. *I lost trust in my parents' ability to support me in a loving and just way.*

I'd lost trust in life—and this became one of my developmental blocks. I was constantly on guard, feeling fearful. Interestingly, Bruce Lipton, a cell biologist, tells us in his article 'Mind over Genes: the new biology' that 'the conscious mind provides 5% or less of the cognitive activity during the day [and] 95–99% of our behaviour is directly derived from the sub-conscious.' So, when your buttons are being pushed it is related back to your original wounding.

Of course, at the time I didn't know that it was a triangle game as such, but I felt the consequences of its destructive behaviour. It became one of my negative core patterns. I grew up wounded, just like my parents, and took those wounds into my marriage, work and relationships. Small groups were always a challenge because I lacked the self-confidence to speak up, I didn't feel safe and feared rejection. Many of us have our own dance-in-a-triangle pattern. It's just with different people, in different situations, but it's the *same dance.*

When I started to study energy medicine and began working on my personal development, I came to understand what was driving my negative patterns. I could now see things differently, take responsibility for myself, and decided to change. Recognising how I had created these same themes in my own family, between my husband and children, was a huge insight. It still took a while for all the twists and turns to emerge: it was like dancing a slow waltz—two steps forward, one to the side and then one back. But I realised then that there was no point blaming my parents—this was *my* life.

Much later I discovered that these patterns stem back to your level of awareness at any given point of time in your life. If you are unaware of your patterns, you can bet your parents were too. I exclude here vicious and violent sexual or physical abuse. All parents are aware of this behaviour. In these instances the patterns require deep transformative psychotherapy.

I have come to realise that what you don't see within you (your inner world) will be reflected and danced outside you in your outer world. You literally pull towards you the necessary people to reflect these same energy patterns back to you, to help you move on.

In the *dance of the drama triangle*, the victim, persecutor and rescuer get locked into manipulative behaviour and personal power issues. There is always suffering at some level for each person. And until you have the ability to recognise these recurring patterns, you will feel powerless to change your position in the triangle, always feeling the victim.

The drama triangle

Let's look at the three roles in the triangle.

If you find yourself in the role of the *persecutor* you are probably trying to control and manipulate the situation to your best advantage. You may be a completely unconscious persecutor, but you are still stepping on other people's toes regardless. Your motive is all about power. The persecutor acts selfishly and generally projects their stuff by using personal will for self-aggrandisement. The persecutor is like an arsonist: deliberately lighting fires, then moving on quickly so they don't get burnt!

For every *victim,* the 'poor me' character who is constantly rejected and dejected, there is a persecutor and rescuer. A victim will always pass responsibility on to a rescuer, never trying to overcome their sense of oppression or feelings of hopelessness, helplessness or powerlessness themselves. They will unconsciously block themselves from making decisions or solving their own problems in order to stay in the victim role. Playing the victim role means you don't have to take responsibility for your actions. (This victim role is not to be confused with the genuine victim that needs loving support and assistance during difficult times.)

Then there is the *rescuer,* who always appears to have good intentions, but in reality has a tendency to seize the opportunity at hand so they can feel good about themselves and satisfy their own unfulfilled needs for power and authority in a hidden way. Their rescuing of others gives them a misplaced sense of importance. Often they too can be wounded and are looking for love and approval. If the victim is completely unaware of the drama dance taking place, they may fall prey to being controlled by the rescuer. A rescuer has a tendency to do more than their fair share in a difficult situation, and can become resentful if they are not rewarded or appreciated.

For those rescuers among us—and I can certainly put my hand up here—you need to find out why you continuously feature in this role. It's a good one to ponder. Rescuers can also end up disempowering the victim by allowing them to always remain a victim, instead of helping them feel empowered, take responsibility for themselves and come out as a winner not a loser.

The winner's triangle

When we align the roles in the drama triangle it becomes the winner's triangle.

In the winner's triangle, the persecutor's manipulation is changed to an *assertive* role. Assertive people ask for what they want and say no to what they don't want. They make the necessary changes to have their needs met and to support themselves.

By doing this, the once-victim now becomes aware of their own feelings and can think and problem-solve for themselves. They understand that it's OK to feel *vulnerable*.

The rescuer's role becomes one of *caring* and empathy; they support but don't take over. They have the skills to listen attentively, allowing the vulnerable player to come to their own levels of awareness about their situation.

You can connect to your own dance of the drama triangle by recognising the key players in your personal dramas, whether it's a love triangle, work triangle, intimate triangle or a sports triangle. Take a step back and reflect on the pattern being played out. You might be surprised at what you find.

If nothing springs to mind immediately, a good place to start is relationships, particularly those of your birth family. Have you ever felt like the meat in the sandwich, caught between two opposing forces? The dance of the drama triangle can feel just like that. Take a look at what's happening for you at work and in your friendships. Are certain themes emerging? This dance touches us all in some way and recognising that equips you to become a better, more positive player in the game of life.

It wasn't until I was able to see my life with my eyes wide open that I fully understood the domino effect of the dance of the drama triangle. Recently I witnessed the kind of injustice that had prevailed in my childhood. I found myself in a time warp, zapped back to the past. I began to re-experience the feelings of seven-year-old Annie standing frozen at the doorway of my brother's childhood room. The same dance was being played out—but now it was in my immediate environment between myself, my husband and my daughter. I could feel my body going into shock, just like all those years ago.

My brother and I were part of the dance of the drama triangle when we were growing up. Both parents were unhappy in their marriage and had many unaddressed family issues that included abuse, deceit, manipulation, control, prejudice, rejection and abandonment. There were plenty of skeletons in the family closet! Because these issues were not addressed they created a tense and volatile atmosphere in our childhood home.

Now, here I was as an adult and my childhood memories were running through my body like a mini tornado. In a split second my unaddressed feelings engulfed me. I experienced an outpouring of the frozen emotions from my seven-year-old self—anger, deep sadness and a feeling of being manipulated and controlled—and it overwhelmed me. I wanted to scream *No!* from the rooftop, as my heart thudded heavily in my chest. Then I suddenly realised that I was seeing the dance of the drama triangle I had been participating in all my life! Finally, I could *step out* to make some new choices in ways to relate, transforming the negative pattern I'd carried for years, perhaps even lifetimes! This was one of those moments where insight, letting go, forgiveness and peace were all wrapped up in one. I could now see the truth. And I could love myself, something I had denied myself for decades—its impact was life changing.

When you are aware of how you've been reacting and can change your negative patterns, you step into the natural flow of life. You become the controller of your destiny. Stepping forward is like an orchestra that has found its conductor: it's empowering. And when you feel empowered, you can make better choices. You can also recognise points of friction, and use them to be wiser and more insightful in your relationships with yourself and others. Now when I hear myself saying 'Enough is enough', I know I'm on the edge of a breakthrough, ready to leave another of my negative patterns behind.

<h1 style="text-align:center">39
Finding your feet</h1>

The best way to discover your core patterns is to notice the negative feelings that arise in certain situations. This helps you to learn a whole lot more about yourself. Simply note these feelings without judging them. When you acknowledge that you get mad, feel hurt or frustrated at particular times, you create a safe space for greater self-knowledge to unfold lovingly without guilt or fear.

A great start is to be brave enough to name your feelings— your anger, sense of injustice, fear or lack of self-worth. These words are messages from your unconscious mind helping to show you what emotions are powering your drama dance. You might even choose to talk to yourself to find out what role you are acting out. This allows your inner child, who was unable to express any feelings at the time of trauma, to finally be heard.

Here are some valuable questions to ask yourself:

❀ When have you found yourself in the exact same position?

❀ Where are you experiencing this feeling in your body?

❀ Can you give this feeling a colour?

❀ Is there an age attached to this feeling?

❀ Can you identify what was being said the first time you felt this way?

❀ Where did this original situation taken place: at home, in the garden, playground, at kindergarten or school?

❀ How did you feel in this situation?

❀ Can you identify any words that might describe how you feel now?

❀ Are you by yourself or with someone?

❀ If someone is with you, what are they saying to you right now?

Asking yourself these questions will help you access the stored cellular memory that contains your hidden personal and professional hurts and traumas. In my own experience I've found it's not uncommon to sense, feel or see a time or picture that relates to the energy block you're facing. Give yourself permission to feel this memory because it will provide you with the link between the incidents that are long forgotten but that continue to impact on your life now. Perhaps it was a situation around the kitchen table or in the school playground. It might even be a situation where you felt unable to reach a parent's expectations. You might have been laughed at or ridiculed in the classroom. Whatever the situation, observe the feeling you still experience now. How do you feel in similar situations today?

There may be a number of layers to this core pattern that need work. You may be travelling along in what appears to be a relatively smooth relationship, when all of a sudden you revert back to the old habits and everything starts to go wrong: your relationship breaks up, and your partner tells you that you're the problem. They promptly move out of your life, often without closure. Aagh!

Once you have got over the initial shock, the next question becomes about how you are attracting or setting yourself up to attract these same situations at work, in relationships and in the family time and time again. You will find the answers by using self-exploration tools like those we've discussed or you might like to find a good energy practitioner who can help you work through this process.

It's useful to know that when you're in the dance of the drama triangle you feel drained, despondent, emotional, out of balance and cynical about relationships in general. There is always an under- or over-compensation of power issues going on as well. You may feel like a mouse in a maze, or you may be on a power trip to cover up your hurt. Either way, these responses aren't helpful to you.

When you enter the dance of the drama triangle in an unhealthy way, you continue the negative patterns of your childhood, and render yourself powerless to activate change. In a way you are victimising yourself. This brings up many unanswered questions about love, particularly the right to sense and feel love in an open and beautiful way. You might even be fearful about relationships altogether. In my experience, I found that it impinged on my ability to nurture myself, and openly and honestly receive love from others. My realisations about my love issues were painful: I saw how I over-nurtured others. But it was only in the seeing that enabled me to move on.

We *all* have the ability to recognise the patterns of our dance and we all have the power to *change* the energy dynamics once they are understood—that's the *gift* and excitement of the journey.

40

Remember the movie

I've always loved the movie *Dances with Wolves* starring Kevin Costner. His character, Lieutenant Dunbar, in many ways was a victim of circumstance, and that led him to the dangerous Western frontier. Sensing the peril of his mission Dunbar quickly realises the key to his survival in the wilderness depends on tracking the movements and habits of a hostile tribe of Native Americans and of a lone wolf who appears eerily on top of a nearby hill.

To alleviate his boredom and the possible onset of insanity through chronic loneliness, Dunbar decides to start a disciplined exercise routine to keep fit and mentally alert. He also takes some time each day to seek out any hidden non-perishable food and ammunition left by previous soldiers. He starts a diary and an ordered system to divide up his daily rations.

Tucked up in the small cabin he now called home, Dunbar starts to make notes of the wolf's timely visits, its habits and inquisitive behaviour. He also notes the frequent visits of a small group of Native Americans who keep an eye on his outpost for any signs of life. It is a cat and mouse game. Dunbar finds great solace in his daily writing and drawings in a small leather-bound diary. Little does he know how valuable this will prove to be!

These recordings provide Dunbar with a much-needed purpose in his isolation. They give his day order and structure. He has to improve his survival skills to live in such harsh conditions. This stretches his abilities as a soldier and as a person.

Time moves on and the hope of a relief party diminishes. His diary entries become his only means of expression for what he sees and feels about the world around him. It becomes habit for him to pour out his feelings in this little book. In a funny sort of way it gives him permission to step beyond the known and learn the value of silence and focus, and to trust the rhythm of nature. There is a time to build and work, to store, rest and play. Over time Dunbar becomes familiar with the patterns and wisdom each season offers. Then he suddenly realises there is a purpose to life and in every living thing, and that nature wastes nothing. He senses the pulse of Mother Earth's immeasurable timing. When he finally surrenders to his new life, he experiences the great freedom it brings to his whole being. Intoxicated by feeling so alive he dances unselfconsciously around the campfire.

In his diary he then writes about the beauty of the stars, moon and sun, the Earth, water and trees. This connection with nature brings a real and tangible purpose to Dunbar's isolation. Now not a victim of circumstance, he no longer fears the wolf or the Native Americans—he is merely curious about them. Out of his isolation comes a beautiful connection with the animal kingdom, and a strong and powerful connection to the indigenous Americans.

He learns to respect their culture, Mother Earth and the great spirit. The Elders of the tribe, his new teachers, instruct him on the importance of timing and patience, and with this knowledge Dunbar feels renewed and alive. He finds his *real* self.

As Dunbar continues his keen observation of the wolf, and his friendship with the native tribes, his own fears pale into insignificance. He finds himself connecting with beauty so deep it enables him to discover a level of courage and wisdom he didn't know he was capable of. He is then able to reach out for solace and companionship with the wolf, which he lovingly calls Two Socks, and is richly rewarded as a result.

Costner's character demonstrates that while our life circumstances may be less than ideal, the challenge is in how you deal with adverse situations, for this is where the real treasure lies. Each time you limit your beliefs and responses, you limit your potential truth and growth. These precious light-bulb moments are filled with possibilities for you to become the kind of person you most want to be.

The magic is, if I can do it— so can you!

In my loneliness and isolation as a child, from my victim of circumstance perspective, I felt threatened and fearful of the world around me. I too had to make friends with death many times over, find my hidden passion and learn to love myself. No experience, good or bad, need ever be lost. The curious thing is that in my fear I became sensitive towards others, and discovered that I could read what was going on for them, even when this was hidden. It was this skill, motivated by self-preservation, fear, loss and insecurity, that now helps me to empower others in their quest for self-healing.

And just like Costner's character, I began to sense that something far greater than myself, something that sustained all life in its wholeness and beauty, was reaching out to me. I began to trust this new world of possibilities and nothing has been the same since.

Recommended reading and resources

Jack Angelo, *Spiritual Healing: A practical guide to hands-on healing*, Godsfield Press, Airesford, 2001

Alice A. Bailey, *Ponder on This*, Lucis Publishing Company, New York and London, 1971

——*The Soul and its Mechansim*, Lucis Publishing Company, New York and London, 1973

——*Initiation Human and Solar*, Lucis Publishing Company, New York and London, 1997

Lama Surya Das, *Awakening the Buddha Within*, Bantam Doubleday Dell Publishing Group, New York, 1997

Ken Dychtwald, *Bodymind*, GP Putnam's Sons, New York, 1997

Dr Masaru Emoto, *The Hidden Messages in Water*, Beyond Words Publishing, Hillsboro, OR, 2004

Jorgen Frydenlund, *Understanding Meridians*, Alterna, Skive, Denmark, 1996

Jennifer Harper ND, PhD, *Nine Ways to Body Wisdom*, Thorsons, Berwick-upon-Tweed, 1997

Judy Jacka, *Synthesis in Healing*, Hampton Roads Publishing Company, Charlottesville, VA, 2003

Anodea Judith, *Eastern Body Western Mind*, Celestial Arts, Berkeley, CA, 2004

Arthur E. Powell, *The Mental Body,* Theosophical Publishing House, Chennai, India, 2000

Sanaya Roman, *Spiritual Growth: Being your Higher Self*, HJ Kramer Inc, Tiburon, CA, 1989

Inna Segal, *The Secret Language of your Body*, Blue Angel Gallery, Glen Waverley, VIC, 2007

Mechthild Scheffer, *The Encyclopedia of Bach Flower Therapy*, Healing Arts Press, Rochester, VT, 2001

Rinpoche Sogyal, *The Tibetan Book of Living and Dying*, Harper, San Francisco, 1992

Dr Randolph Stone, *The Polarity Process*, Element Books, Dorset, UK, 1989

Ian White, *Bush Flower Healing*, Bantam, Sydney, 1999

White Eagle, *Spiritual Unfoldment 1–4*, White Eagle Publishing Trust, Liss, UK, 1942

——*The Light Bringer*, White Eagle Publishing Trust, Liss, UK, 2001

Electronic resources

Australian Bush Flower Essences: <www.ausflowers.com.au>
Bach Flower Remedies: <www.bachflower.com>
The Energetic Healers Association: <www.energetichealing.org.au>
Findhorn Flower Essences: <www.findhornessences.com>

Printed in Dunstable, United Kingdom